Like
A River Glorious

Gavin Barnett

WIPF & STOCK · Eugene, Oregon

Wipf and Stock Publishers
199 W 8th Ave, Suite 3
Eugene, OR 97401

Like A River Glorious
By Barnett, G. G.

ISBN 13: 978-1-59244-860-9
ISBN: 1-59244-860-7
Publication date 9/13/2004
Previously published by The Mantech Organisation cc, 2004

Like A River Glorious

CONTENTS

Preface

In a significant speech to the South African parliament during 1960, Harold Macmillan announced that "the winds of change were sweeping across Africa". Reaching gale force in British colonial Africa almost immediately, these winds consigned many of the customs, cultures and conditions of a century or more, to a bygone era in less than four years.

The two pillars of what Europeans perceived as civilisation, namely the British civil service and the mostly altruistic missionaries, were suddenly virtually irrelevant.

The familiar District Commissioner, whose authority carried the full might of British law including the power to administer capital punishment, his District Officer and horde of indigenous saluting and fez-wearing 'messengers' became instantly anachronistic.

The haste to shed responsibility for African colonies with its acquired political stigma, was matched only by the speed with which the concept of *Uhuru* gained traction among colonised people.

Dedicated missionaries most of whom having sacrificed comfort and career, risked malaria, sunstroke and other hazards to bring the gospel, medicine and education to the dark continent, were in many cases treated as redundant. This development was unfair especially to non-conformist missions which had always encouraged a degree of self-governance in the church. Missions with a more centralised, rigid structure and dogma were, un-surprisingly better able to maintain their wonted control a little longer.

To argue that despite many mistakes and some harsh treatment, the colonial era did bestow considerable benefits on Africa, had become politically incorrect. The urge to retreat from imperialism gained strength because of the vogue towards democracy which would supposedly solve all of Africa's problems. In practical terms, the economic and cultural costs of staying on another generation or two in the hope that Africa might eventually absorb Western civilised values, develop a work ethic and give up tribalism, had become distinctly prohibitive. Yet some brave souls did exactly that.

In this narrative I have frequently referred to the indigenous people of Africa as natives. This is the term used by my father Fred in his diary and my mother Dorothy in correspondence, without an iota of disrespect or racism and has, at least, the advantage of being accurate.

In the decades that have followed a number of terms have been used including "natives" which have often been perceived as pejorative. Indeed even the terms preferred during the nineteen sixties by Americans of African descent, such as "blacks", later became politically incorrect.

This latter term obviously does not mingle well with the Christian concept of "black hearts" needing to be "washed whiter than the snow". Depiction of sin as black, the scriptural statement that "men love darkness rather than light because their deeds are evil" and the phrase "darkest Africa", today, fall into this sensitive category.

Missionaries who remained, found themselves facing vastly changed attitudes both in regard to church governance and their personal status as community leaders.

In the political realm, the indigenous people had espoused the idea that they would be better off without the "yoke" of colonialism and their leaders were eager to enjoy the leisure and wealth that was expected to come automatically with political power.

As a 'missionary kid', and a raconteur from that bygone era, who has enjoyed captivating his spellbound listeners with stories of his boyhood in Northern Rhodesia, I have been prevailed upon to contribute to the record, before so much is forgotten and consigned to the mists of time.

Above all, however, this book is a biography of my mother, Dorothy Barnett, a remarkably courageous and talented missionary, nurse, teacher and parent who, as a widow with four children younger than 5 years, set a unique example of commitment to her faith, tenacity in the face of thanklessness, courage in the presence of danger and an effervescent sense of humour when so many saw only grim gloom and solemnity.

The powerful influence of the mighty Zambezi river in tragedy and survival, in fear and tranquillity, together with some lines from one of Mother's favourite old hymns, combine to provide a symbolic imagery for the biography. The variety of the Zambezi's moods, its rapids, still waters, dangers and beauty are seen as analogous to the vicissitudes of Mother's life and give rise to the book title: *Like a River Glorious.*

The hymn known by that title was written by Frances R. Havergal (1836-1879) to a composition by J. Mountain which he named *Wye Valley*, inspired by the beautiful river of that name.

(http://www.tagnet.org/digitalhymnal/en/dh074.html).

The frequently mentioned "Children of Chavuma" are my brother

Walter and twin sisters Dorothy and Margaret as well as Frances,

Esther, Eleanor, Viola, Grace, Paul and David; sons and daughters of the wonderful Logan family, who shared a unique experience and benefited from a valuable common heritage. In a broader sense, the description refers also to the many hundreds of childlike people who were blessed in material or spiritual ways by their contact with my mother.

Humour enabled her, at times, to strike a balance between the ideals of exegetical and orthodox theology and the practical situations that often confronted us.

Since even this lady's sense of humour could on occasion be a little irreverent, a tendency also highly developed in most missionary kids, the impish approach I have used in telling the story should not be altogether unexpected.

One does not have to concur totally with the theological views of one's parents in order to love and respect them, to appreciate their extraordinary strength of character, ability and achievements, or to benefit from the example they set and the heritage they bequeathed.

The pleasing demand for this publication has prompted this third edition. A few of the unsolicited responses from readers in seven continents are quoted in the Epilogue.

GGB

1. The Lady who became NyaKapalu

It was just before midnight. The absence of any artificial light lent brightness to the starry sky. The African drums that had beaten incessantly at the ritual dance in the village across the river, were now silent. The cry of a wild dog and the eerie call of the night jar indicated that nocturnal creatures were on the prowl. Mosquito nets tucked in, the family slept.

A loud knocking on the door woke her. Nyakapalu lit a paraffin lantern, put on a night gown and hastened to the door.

Opening it she saw two native men standing by a crudely assembled stretcher on which lay a women bleeding and moaning in agony. The woman had been mauled by a crocodile while swimming in the Zambezi and pulling a woven fishing basket through the water to catch minnows. After some treatment from the village medicine man they had carried her the long journey to the foot of Chavuma hill and then struggled up the stony, winding footpath to Chavuma mission station.

By the light of the flickering lantern, she could see the wounds were severe and the crude herb and clay plaster applied by the traditional healer seemed likely to hasten sepsis.

She told the men to take the patient up the road to the mission dispensary. Waking five-year-old Kapalu, her eldest son, she explained the situation and followed the bearers out into the dark night carrying a hurricane lantern and her medical encyclopaedia. A number of night prowlers scuttled away into the blackness as she walked up the road. Hyenas, often around, were silent this night.

At the dispensary, NyaKapalu supplied a mild sedative, removed the medicine man's sticky cocktail, bathed the wounds in an antiseptic liquid and applied suitable dressings. One of the round thatched huts near the dispensary served as accommodation. Further attention could wait until morning.

After offering a prayer in the Lwena language for physical and spiritual healing, the missionary walked back through the tropical night down to her house, the swinging lantern casting grotesque shadows on the pathway.

All was well and soon the household slept once more. This was not an entirely rare event as these chronicles describe.

Who was this lady they called Nyakapalu, meaning 'mother of Kapalu' and what was she doing in a remote and inhospitable area of tropical Africa far away from her relatives and home in Melbourne, Victoria?

As Kapalu and author of these chronicles, let me begin the story in that Australian city in the year 1898.

Edward Oscar Sandbach, son of Walter, one of the discoverers of gold in Bendigo, lived at 56 Crown Street, Flemington, Melbourne.

> With two of my own sons Rod and Geoff, I visited Bendigo, Victoria in June 2002. Here the gold mine museum records much information about the brothers Walter and William Sandbach who discovered and panned for alluvial gold in the stream to the sound of Cuckabarras in 1851. Rod, Geoff and I pilgrimaged overnight at the homestead known as Ravenswood built 1857 on the farm where the Sandbach brothers had operated as shepherds in the nineteenth century.

Edward Sandbach had three sons and a daughter named Dorothy Agnes

Sandbach who was born on 23rd Nov 1898. Her mother Margaret, maiden name Webster, died quite young after the birth of their children Walter, Keith and Dorothy.

Edward's second wife slipped easily into the classical stepmother mould, often being unfair to the three siblings, especially after the birth of her own son Albert. At times Dorothy was hungry and miserable. She told me, about 24 years later, how, having been sent to the shop by her stepmother whom they called "the lady", to buy a loaf of fresh bread, Dorothy had been so hungry she had not been able to resist the delicious aroma of freshly baked bread, and started to nibble at the crust on the way home.

Human nature prevailed and as the little girl entered the gate she realised in panic that the crust had been conspicuously eroded, so that shame and punishment inevitably lay in store for her. "The lady" fulfilled Dorothy's worst apprehensions, showing no mercy and causing tears to flow.

A year or two later, events proved that the stepmother was neither honest, nor even a lady for that matter and together with Albert, who had been under her expert tuition, had to face the wrath of the law over stolen goods. From that time Dorothy, Walter and Keith were made wards of the court and brought up by their aunt, Edward's sister Sarah.

Dorothy inherited her father's musical talent and had a beautiful singing voice. As she grew up her blonde wavy hair turned dark, framing a face of classical beauty. She had to begin earning quickly and started work as a learner dressmaker, little realising how well the skill would serve her later, pedalling a treadle sewing machine in darkest Africa.

Brought up as a Presbyterian, she developed a strong faith and became captivated by the vision of missionary work. The determined young dressmaker managed to undertake a two year theological diploma course at the Melbourne Bible Institute founded by Anglican clergyman, Dr C. H. Nash in 1920 and now the Bible College of Victoria.

It was there she met Fred Barnett a young dedicated student. Common interests in the Christian faith and in music, doubtless played a role in their romance and engagement, by which time they were both committed to missionary careers.

Dorothy Sandbach 1927

One of the Melbourne Bible Institute's later students Bishop Stephen Bradley was sent as a missionary to Natal, South Africa in 1936 and retired in Cape Town until his death in 2003.
Though he never actually met Dorothy Barnett, Stephen Bradley remembers the Institute's principal Dr C. H. Nash in the early1930's thirties, frequently commending Dorothy Barnett to his students as a fine example of what a missionary should be.

Having maintained correspondence with Fred and Dorothy, Nash had been aware of the example of personal commitment and fortitude set by this extraordinary couple in the story that is to follow.

The pages of a Scofield Bible given to Dorothy by Fred on 28th October 1924 while at the Institute, are annotated with her comments as an earnest Biblical student.

Nursing her aunt Sarah who by then was terminally ill, Dorothy had been unable to accompany her fiancé Fred, on 1st May 1926 when, as a young ardent missionary-printer of 23 years, he sailed for Africa.

My mother, the talented Dorothy Sandbach, called NyaKapalu by the natives of central Africa, is the central figure in this tale of purpose and courage and of boyhood adventures in which the great Zambezi river played such a pervasive role.

Perhaps it is because the legendary waterway is woven so vividly into the tapestry of my mother's life that a symbolic association comes so naturally to the writer.

At its source the Zambezi springs from the side of a low hill the other side of which is the source of the Congo river. A drop of rain falling on the hill is destined capriciously to join many other drops flowing either into the Atlantic Ocean via the Congo river or divergently into the Indian Ocean after careering adventurously along the Zambezi.

The watershed in Mother's life was probably the decision to study at the Melbourne Bible Institute or perhaps it was a spiritual experience which prompted her missionary vision.

Forfeiting a potentially successful career in material terms, willingly relinquishing the opportunity of a comfortable lifestyle and the enjoyment of exercising her musical and other talents in a civilised, healthy and safe environment amongst friends and relatives, she never swerved from her calling.

Mere intellectual acquiescence to the tenets of Christianity could never produce commitment of this order. It is difficult, in human terms, to explain the sacrifice and commitment displayed by the heroine of this story.

Her life was indeed 'like a glorious river' meandering in pleasant meadows, splashing through rapids, roaring majestically over great falls or slowing deep and dark. Traversing forbidding and threatening territory, startled by the unexpected around a corner, often mercifully tranquil and always sustaining others.

Hers was the kind of determination and tenacity that remains undeterred on finding that the more glamorous visions of mission work among the heathen are unrealistic, that a mission of any help at all necessarily involves sacrifices, the hazards of the climate, disease and danger from wild animals and reptiles.

The goal of this dedication was to bring the Christian Gospel to heathen people, who were largely hunter-gatherers, in many cases still belonged to an iron-age culture, and employed witchcraft in practising extremely cruel behaviour towards aged villagers who had outlived their usefulness.

While the main task was the propagation of the Gospel, medical care was provided as a way to exemplify Christian virtue and basic education was provided to permit reading of the Bible which the missionaries translated into the local languages, having first devised a phonetic writing system for them.

This commitment did in addition, extend to carrying out effectively, all the responsibilities of bringing up a family in a foreign and dangerous part of the world, far from schools, libraries, shops, doctors, banks and many of the basic living facilities we mostly take for granted.

The chronicle now introduces my father Fred Barnett, the energetic man who became SaKapalu (father of Kapalu).

2. Printer, Pastor and Preacher.

The original diary penned by my father, Frederick Mitchell Barnett, covers a period of twelve months from 1st May 1926. The entry for that day reads:

"Set sail from Williamstown for Durban at 5.00pm. Boat left 5 hours late. Had dinner on shore with a gathering of 17 relations etc. Friends sang "Trust and Obey" as boat moved off. Smooth voyage down the bay. Rough through the rip. The pilot ship a beautiful sight lit up. Interesting to see the pilot change boats. Passed through the rip approximately 8.30. Having a good sea-saw time outside the heads. How much to praise God for - "Kept by his power".

Born 5th November 1900 of Daniel Mitchell and Mary Anne (nee Bissett) in the city of Hawthorn, colony of Victoria, Australia, my father Fred had two brothers William and Alfred and a sister Margaret.

Alfred it was who later donated a bronze bust of their grandfather William, to the City of Avoca where he had been magistrate, gold trader, retailer and mayor during the latter half of the nineteenth century.

> With two of my sons Rod and Geoff, I visited Avoca in 2003 and stood in the magistrate's rostrum where William had passed many a sentence, walked along Barnett street and saw his retail store now a Post Office.

Fred Barnett had the gift of the gab. As a boy he would come rushing in to his mother Mary where they lived at 68 Argyle Street, Moonie Ponds, Melbourne, bursting with news. So excited was he by some event or idea, that even his normally excellent verbal facility could not match his eagerness to relate the story. It would tumble out in a breathless jumble of words.

Fred won a medal for fielding in cricket and later became a scout-master. He had decided on a printing career and, after qualifying, enrolled on 16th September 1924 to study for two years at the Melbourne Bible Institute. It was there he met the attractive and capable Dorothy Sandbach. Their romance blossomed, they became engaged and decided to "heed a call" to the African mission field.

Writing on 16th October 1934, ten years later, Dorothy reveals how this call came. Fred had attended a missionary conference at Camberwell Hall, Melbourne, to hear a man, named Johnston, speak about a mission press in Roodepoort, a mining town near Johannesburg, South Africa. The Roodepoort Mission Press was, housed in a corrugated iron building located among the dusty sand dumps on the property of the Durban Roodepoort Deep Mine.

The objective of the press was to print gospel tracts in English, Afrikaans and in those indigenous languages such as Xhosa, Zulu and seven others, for which an alphabet had been developed. Christian missionaries played an enormous role in developing a written language and producing books for African people many of whom even by the twentieth century had not themselves developed writing of their own.

Johnson was Honorary Secretary of the mission press and fellow-shipped with the Brethren, sometimes called the Plymouth Brethren. Fred was not at the time associated with them though he had met Brethren students at the Bible Institute.

Much will be said about this evangelical Christian movement in these chronicles but it might be appropriate at this point to quote an extract from the web site www.brethrenonline.org :

Fred M. Barnett 1926

"In the 1820's, a small group of Christians met in an attempt to return to New Testament simplicity. They took as their guide, not the creeds and religious traditions of the denominations around them, but rather the Bible. Through many growing pains and some setbacks, their spiritual example is alive and growing today. These Christians have been called by many names - Plymouth Brethren being sometimes used. But their true allegiance remains the Lord Jesus Christ, and they seek happy fellowship with all Christian brethren who love the Lord and seek to follow His word".

After graduating, Fred was selected by Africa Golden Harvests to relieve the incumbent missionary printer W.J. Kerr in the work of printing Gospel tracts. Mr Kerr's health was failing and the press needed upgrading.

Fred's diary, supplemented by letters he wrote while at sea,

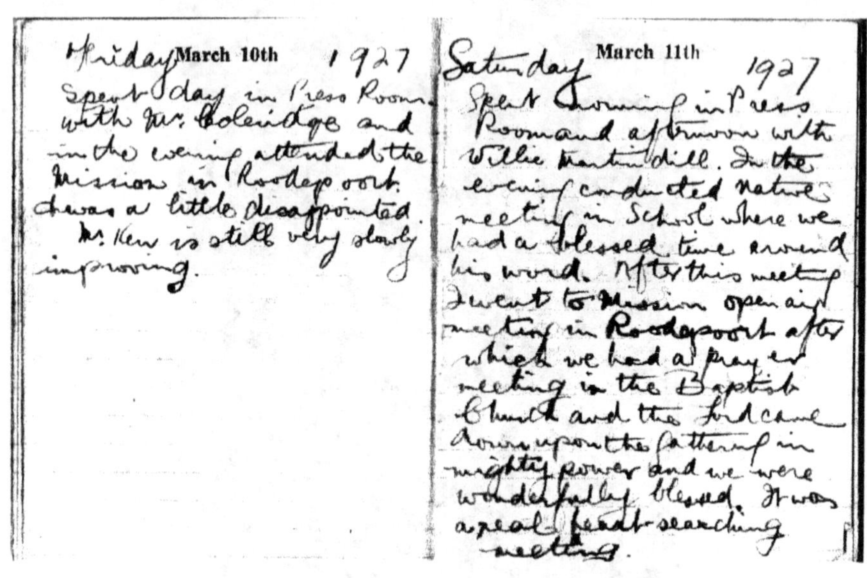

Friday March 10th 1927

Spent day in Press Room with Mr. Coleridge and in the evening attended the Mission in Roodepoort. I was a little disappointed. Mr. Kew is still very slowly improving.

Saturday March 11th 1927

Spent morning in Press Room and afternoon with Willie [illegible]. In the evening conducted native meeting in School where we had a blessed time around his word. After this meeting I went to Mission open air meeting in Roodepoort after which we had a prayer meeting in the Baptist Church and the Lord came down upon the gathering in mighty power and we were wonderfully blessed. It was a real heart-searching meeting.

Pages of the Diary of Fred Barnett
covering the period 1st May 1926 to 30th April 1927

indicate he had begun his missionary role with vigour even before landing in Africa. He organised and spoke at Gospel meetings aboard the S.S. Berrima and writes enthusiastically of people whom he believed he had helped spiritually during the voyage.

S.S. *Berrima* docked in Durban on Thursday 27th May 1926 and two days later the diary records: *"Had a tiring night in the train (from Durban) to arrive at Johannesburg. Arrived at Roodepoort at approximately 12.30".* Dutifully he sent a cable by Reuters special service informing Hon. Secretary Johnston of his safe arrival.

The diary goes on to record that on the same Saturday, after looking around the press which was to be his home and work base, he conducted a service in the mine compound through a translator after which many came back to the house to sing hymns.

Having not yet rested from the train journey, he then had a meeting with his "*printing assistants, Thomas Mtimkulu and Paulos*".

Enthusiasm and energy characterised this man with a mission. The diary repeatedly expresses gratitude that "*there is much work to do*".

Two days after arriving on the Reef his diary records that after attending a service of the Brethren in Elim Hall, he spoke at two separate services and thereafter attended another service at the Railway Mission arriving back at his new home in Roodepoort at 10.15 pm, admittedly "*tired*".

Four days later on Monday 31st May, he writes of his printing skills:

"I praise God that He has not allowed me to lose any of the art since I left the profession to train in the Melbourne Bible Institute".

By the end of that year a school was started on the property for which both practical and financial help was given by the Brethren Christians in their personal capacities. The respected names of Alf Gibbs and George Leslie are mentioned in the diary in this connection. A number of the trustees of the Mission Press were prominent Brethren Christians like W.J.Coleridge, who gave considerable personal time and support to the mission.

Within months Fred had taken over the press, started a Sunday School, persuaded the Durban Roodepoort Deep management to let him conduct services on their premises and had become active in the distribution of the literature he printed. He records that "*our tracts are being used in the mission societies in Tanganyika and Central Africa*".

He also started learning Zulu, meantime using an Ethiopian interpreter for services he conducted. He writes of employee problems with

"Paulos getting into debt and Thomas relocating to Swaziland". He mentions devising efficient methods for saving labour and print paper. *"We hope to maintain and probably increase our output despite the dearth of labour."*

Besides his full-time job, Fred also did work for the Railway Mission and was appointed to give lectures under the auspices of the Transvaal Bible School Union. He visited leper asylums including the one on Robben Island which accommodated white and black lepers. Visiting that island, just off Cape Town in 2006, I was shown the former office of the Leprosy Mission where Fred had worked.

There is a strong missionary tone throughout the writing. The picture emerges of a dedicated young man of 27 imbued with a sense of mission, destiny and the will of God. He became popular as a gifted preacher and while continuing in fellowship with the Baptist Church and other denominations at whose services he frequently preached, both the support for the Press from the Brethren and Fred's respect for their biblically-based approach to Christian teaching, drew him closer to that denomination.

The Brethren of course preferred not to be described as a denomination. They were "the Lord's people". To some this appeared arrogant but, in fact, to the Brethren it was more an expression of dismay that denominations and factions had crept into the church. Most of the Brethren genuinely welcomed any baptised believer to worship with "the Lord's people".

The Jeppe New Year's Day Conference mentioned in the diary on 1st January 1927, was an annual Brethren event held in Elim Hall, Johannesburg.

Frequently the diary and letters record Fred's conviction that *"Dorothy was the right choice for a bride and that the work he was doing was the will of God".*

Fred's incredible God consciousness did not blunt his practical skills. He improved the press operation, installing new equipment and distinguished himself as a tract writer and printer. In his letter of 12th April 1927 he reports having secured a new electric press able to deliver 2000 prints per hour compared with the old manual machine which managed 1000 prints per day. The cost was donated by the trustees, and Durban Roodepoort Deep Mine management agreed to supply electric power and install the motor without cost.

The motivation of the man is impressive. For many the printing press and its development would have been more than a full time job. Fred hardly missed a day without conducting a gospel or devotional meeting or visiting the natives on the mine to help in their spiritual growth. He travelled all over the Witwatersrand, especially the West Rand, either taking meetings, distributing tracts or attending to the needs of the press.

In a lengthy report in November 1927 he refers to impostor preachers among the natives who were themselves *"not saved"* and had been *"preaching trash".* He mentions with considerable concern, hearing one cleric telling his congregation about how "Pharaoh had tried to kill Jesus". When asked for the supporting Bible passage the cleric said *"he'd lost the place and couldn't find it again".*

In common with mining areas anywhere in the world, there were rough characters and criminals along the Gold Reef. One night returning late from a day of travel, preaching and counselling, Fred saw the glint of a gun barrel pointed at him. A nervous finger tensed on the trigger. He spoke calmly to the man holding the weapon as if this was just another member of his needy flock, and enquired whether he could help. The would-be assailant lowered his gun and disappeared into the darkness.

Significantly the diary's closing entry on Sunday 30th April 1927 refers to a new 'assembly' started by him and reads:

"Had first breaking of bread meeting this morning and 33 sat at the Lord's Table. Praise God. In afternoon Mr Mofidge addressed a full school of natives and we had a fine gospel meeting. Mr Mofidge was impressed. In the evening we had breaking of bread in the native school. God blessed us. Had a talk tonight with an unbeliever. God was working in his heart. Praise God for a splendid day. He answered prayer".

Later in these chronicles we have cause to compare this man to the Biblical character Enoch, because of what might seem to some, a fanatically spiritual devotion to his Master.

When Dorothy Sandbach's aunt, Sarah, passed away the missionary bride of 30 was free to join Fred, then 27, in Africa.

My sister Dorothy has a bible given to Mother by the "Girls of the Flemington Bible Class" in September 1927 as a farewell gift just before she left for Africa. Her arrival in Johannesburg was a memorable day for the dedicated and happy couple.

Fred and Dorothy were married on 21st Jan 1928 in Elim Hall, Fairview, Johannesburg. The marriage officer was Gavin H. Mowat the founder of Chavuma Mission station in central Africa. The denomination on the marriage certificate reads "Plymouth Brethren".

Dorothy's letter to Mr Nash of 8th Feb 1928 refers to her landing in Africa, the many friends who showed kindness, and the secretarial tasks she immediately took up for the work of the press and allied services on the mine premises. She writes: *"We will stay at the Mission House for the present as this is where the work is".*

On 1st January 1929 I was born in the house which doubled as Mission Press and home for the Barnetts. I was named Gavin after Gavin Mowat who officiated as marriage officer for my parents.

In what one might call the "missionary industry", the children of missionaries were frequently dubbed missionary kids, "M.K.'s" for short. I suppose being born in the room next door to the print room, while the "modern" 1927 model machine, clicked away printing out Gospel tracts, ought to be a convincing entitlement to the term.

Of course being an M.K. was not itself any kind of guarantee of potential to become a missionary. Mother held that, to be credible, the missionary "call" must necessarily be individual and personal and not merely a way of life into which an M.K. slips through parental influence alone.

However there were some M.K.'s who did not only follow in the footsteps of their missionary parents but, as second generation missionaries, have since displayed the same outstanding courage and devotion.

Recently after hearing some of the adventures related in this story, and following a query as to whether a missionary career had ever appealed to me, a business colleague remarked: "But Gavin is a missionary of another kind".

This was a reference to the fact that while this M.K. did not make his career in the kind of "mission field" described in this book, I often found myself exerting an inherited aptitude to strive for justice in the face of unfairness, egotism and bullying. This proclivity no doubt learned from my parents, had its adventures too and in recent years led to my founding a small company named Whistleblowers and Performance Brokers whose mission is fairness and justice, which assists victims of corruption and tries to promote transactions in which delivery is given in "good measure, pressed down, shaken together and running over".

Wedding of Fred and Dorothy Barnett 21st January 1928

There are several references in my father's diary, to feeling more than ever that he was *"in the place of the Lord's choosing".* He found himself enjoying the opportunities for preaching and counselling for which he had aptitudes and which clearly provided an alternative to the printing work. It is obvious too that he had been impressed by, and made friends among the Brethren.

As a theological student, he had been familiar with the Brethren doctrinal approach, and the Brethren control of the Roodepoort Mission Press was naturally an important factor in his relationship with them. His increasing connection with Brethren circles seemed to have been generated, by their practical assistance and encouragement in the work of the press, their scripturally-based approach to dogma as distinct from man-made creed or liturgy, and the fact that his own preaching was much in demand among them.

It is clear that, without in any way neglecting the primary responsibility of the press, my father increasingly enjoyed the broader evangelical and pastoral work for which he was obviously gifted.
This does perhaps make it easier to understand what happened next.

3. Call to Chavuma

The metaphorical river of my mother's life had thus far been flowing swiftly, even smoothly and apparently according to divine plan.

By the year 1930 most of the civilised world was in the grip of a severe economic depression. A second M.K., my brother Walter, (perpetuating the pioneering Sandbach name), had arrived making four mouths to feed. The Press had been upgraded and the quality and efficiency of its output vastly improved. A thriving supplementary mission work had been established.

Was this the time to move to other pastures? Was the Mission Press after all only temporarily the *"place of the Lord's choosing"?* Did broader pastoral mission work offer greater scope for the talents of this devout couple?

My father's letter dated 18th March 1930 to Dr. Nash, written perhaps significantly, not from Roodepoort, but from the home of senior missionary Gavin Mowat, then in Johannesburg, announced a surprising decision.

He wrote: *"Dorothy and I have passed through deep waters and because of this we have felt not up to much correspondence. We praise God that through it all we have felt his loving care. As you may have possibly heard we have found it necessary to resign from the work at Roodepoort. This we did only after much earnest thought and prayerful consideration. Second Corinthians 12 verse 9 amply describes our experience"*.

Examination of this scriptural passage and context reveals that the Epistle writer had suffered "reproaches, persecutions and distresses" at the hands of his fellow Christians.

My father's reference to "deep waters" resonates how appropriately the capricious nature of the river symbolises their lives. Signs of turbulence ruffled the surface. Rapids lay ahead and the river was taking a sharp bend as it radically changed direction.

Discovering this correspondence, a lifetime later, brought to mind my mother's having referred only once to an attitude of envy and discourtesy at times displayed towards them by the Kerrs, especially after Mother's arrival and her marriage.

Mr. Kerr's health had been failing, as recorded in a concerned letter by my father, and it seems that Johnston's departure as Honorary Secretary may have left a command vacuum where, even in such a devout atmosphere, a measure of arbitration or discipline might have made a difference.

This reconstruction of the background is reinforced by a paragraph in the same letter to Dr. Nash.

"Often we have thought of your words in the Class room, that 'workers with whom one is associated on the field are often the hardest to work with'. This unfortunately has been our experience. Bro. Kerr is a brother who must work alone and is not happy in harness. Neither Dorothy nor I bear any malice whatsoever and the work at Roodepoort is borne up in prayer continually by us".

My father mentions significantly, that: *"the elder brethren of the various assemblies have met many times to consider the matter of our call to the Interior. Now after much prayer and waiting we hold a document stating that our brethren believe the Lord has called us to this field and they unanimously commend us most heartily to this work."*

He continues: *"The particular place the Lord has laid on our hearts is Chavuma, Northern Rhodesia (the district is known as Lovaleland). There is a great need for the Gospel. It is near the Portuguese Angola border and the natives (Valwena) are purely pagan untouched by the Gospel except in the vicinity of the various mission stations. This tribe of native is pouring in from Portuguese territory and settling largely in the district we hope (D. V.) to go to. We hope to leave for Chavuma early in July. We go by train to Livingstone 3 or 4 days and then take a barge on the Zambezi river journeying up for approximately six weeks We are in fellowship with the Christian Brethren and it is to a station carried on by them we are going".*

He mentions the help and fellowship of Gavin Mowat who founded Chavuma station and who, in Johannesburg for the education of his seven children, was busy translating the Bible into the Lwena language and helping the Barnetts to start learning the language even before leaving.

W. J. Coleridge, the very great friend, supporter and trustee of the Mission Press, decided to resign from association with the press, at the same time.

On 19th June 1930 the Acting Secretary replied to the letter of resignation in understanding terms, making it clear that my father's reputation in the mission and among supporters in Australia, was not affected and that his decision to move north was approved.

The boldness of this move may not be apparent to many. The Barnetts were moving away from a mission with more or less formal financial structures in Australia and strong support from South African trustees, to, what the Brethren called, a life of faith; an accurate description since Brethren missionaries enjoyed no stipend or guarantee of support other than those promised in scripture.

While this unexpected change, in what seemed a divinely ordained plan, could be the subject of human debate, it is certain that my parents were utterly sincere and had no doubt in their minds that they were now obeying God's command in 1930 to move northwards into tropical Africa.

Father's letter mentions the mode of travel, acquisition of his cottage tent, the daily dose of quinine, a mosquito net, a shot gun and rifle, all of which would be *"useful from the day they arrived at the banks of the Zambezi"*. He mentions the rifle as being needed for *"self protection and a change of meat diet occasionally"*. The shot gun was to save my life just a year or so later.

And so began the long journey by steam train from Johannesburg through Bechuanaland Protectorate (now Botswana) to Livingstone in Northern Rhodesia (now Zambia). At Livingstone, my parents with their sons Gavin and Walter embarked by barge propelled by skilled paddlers on an epic journey up the mighty Zambezi river to Chavuma.

This mode of travel, its breath-taking scenery and cruel hazards are described more fully elsewhere in these chronicles.

The barge powered by 16, now tired, paddlers plunging their paddles in unison under the direction of a skilled *kapitano* and carrying its new missionary family, had moved up-stream steadily for six weeks in the wildest of terrains, camping nightly, traversing hazardous cataracts and coping with all the special domestic needs of two babies about to become children of Chavuma.

As the barge turned the last of many scenically beautiful corners, the impressive Chavuma falls came into view a kilometre upstream. Its thundering torrent in a spectacular water spout, poured into the calmer waters of the broad basin that served as a crossing and landing beach for dugout canoes and barges.

The Barnett Family en route to Chavuma

On the sandy shore a crowd waited. The four resident missionaries, their families and about 100 natives began waving and singing in welcome as the barge turned out of the main current towards the beach.

Seeing the welcoming crowd, the paddlers in a display of showmanship dipped their paddles even deeper into the water in perfect unison increasing power and speed and occasionally ecstatically lashing the surface to produce dramatic spurts of spray. One grand forward thrust beaching the barge high up on the shore, ended the theatrical flurry.

It was the end of October 1930 and the Barnett family had arrived at Chavuma.

4. *Chavuma - It roars!*

Seventy-five kilometres along the great river, northwards from Balovale, (now a town called Zambezi) lies the formidable cataract *Chavuma*, "it roars".

Two gigantic ridges of volcanic rock protruding from the east and west banks all but meet in the centre, leaving a narrow gap of about thirty metres through which the mighty Zambezi, known locally as *Yambeji,* has to force its entire volume under pressure. The effect is a grand water spout belching horizontally at first and then dropping some 5 metres into the river below. Here the river widens to about one kilometre.

Despite the distance across and some swift and unpredictable currents, the point below the falls was chosen as a regular canoe crossing. When the Zambezi comes down in flood draining a large area of central Africa, the river at this crossing is turbulent and for some distance below the water spout itself, the spray and waves might soon fill a small and unstable dugout.

In recent times the cataract has been selected as a point to measure the flow volume providing reliable data for forecasting the Barotseland and Kariba summer flood levels. There is an established correlation between the cusecs measured at Chavuma and the Kariba level a few months later.

Chavuma mission was established on one of three prominent, wooded hills, on the eastern bank about 3 kilometres up-river from the Chavuma falls, and ten kilometres south of the Angolan border, on the 13° 0' latitude South and longitude 22° 42' East.

The founding of the mission station in 1923 is associated with respected names of Gavin Mowat and Bert Sims.

The jutting section of the Angolan boundary had been settled in talks between Cecil John Rhodes and the Portuguese colonial authority, who had accused Britain of leaving them nothing of the Zambezi. Rhodes, the story goes, took a pen and magnanimously drew a line eastwards along the 13° latitude South, as far as the Manyinga river and then a line following various rivers northwards to the Belgian Congo, at a spot just north of the Zambezi source, where today's boundaries of Zambia, the D.R.C. and Angola meet.

With the stroke of a pen he had excised from the British colony, a 500 km stretch of the Zambezi running northwards from a village called Chingi, where Chavuma mission later established an out- school.

For a denomination that had no creed, headquarters or organisational structure, the Brethren missionary effort made a powerful impact all over the world. In central Africa, Brethren established more missions than any protestant denomination or Roman Catholic order.

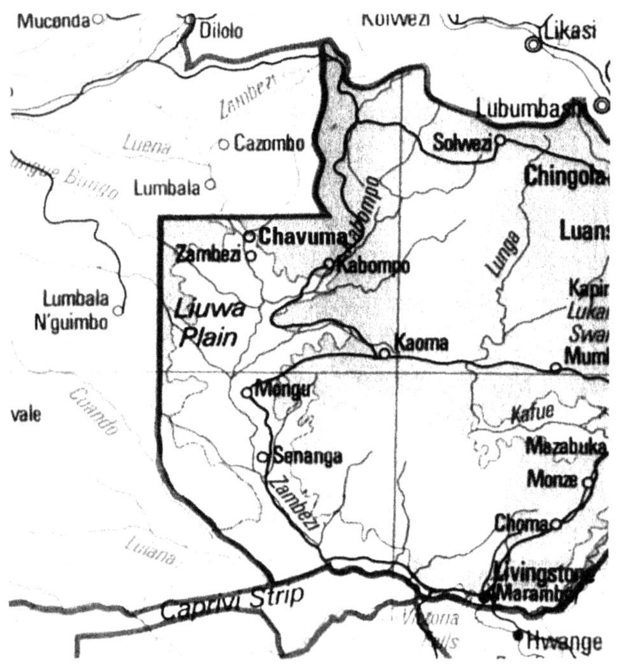

A map of the Chavuma region

A rectangle across the continent between the latitudes 5° North and 20° South of the Equator became known in Brethren circles as "The Beloved Strip".

This is remarkable in the light of the recorded fact that apart from a small minority of self supporting missionaries among them, no Brethren missionary enjoyed a regular stipend or allowance or indeed any guarantee of financial support or rescue. The "life of faith" was not a totally new concept to Fred and Dorothy, though that faith was going to be severely tested.

A minimum element of administrative organisation existed in the form of the Australian Missionary Tidings, the title of a journal which informed Brethren of the activities of Australian missionaries around the world and which pooled certain voluntary donations for 'fair' distribution among the needy ones. The Brethren, who were at pains to avoid being seen as just one more denomination or sect, used a general title "Christian Missions in Many Lands" as label for their impressive missionary effort.

The A.M.T. continue their good work in modern times from an office in Eastwood, Sydney which I had the privilege of visiting in June 2002. The AMT has since moved to Brisbane, Queensland. Their quarterly news journals between the years 1935 and 1943 contain some forty letters written by my mother, who was first listed as a Brethren missionary in the February 1935 issue.

Before the arrival of David Livingstone and the colonialists, the native tribes had not settled themselves as separate countries. Notional, unmapped territories were claimed but not always observed by the separate tribes. Being marked by the constantly encroaching edge of the forest or bush that remained un-cleared, village boundaries were more visible and defensible than territorial borders which were largely a colonially imposed concept.

While several villages of the same tribe tended to exist as neighbours, any given stretch of territory in the North Western province of N. Rhodesia, might accommodate villages of Lwena, Lunda, Chokwe or Luchaji tribes.

This is illustrated by the fact that there are two widely separated tributaries of the Zambezi named Lwena, one flowing in from the west in what became known as Angola and another from the eastern side in Northern Rhodesia. Historically, different parts of the Lwena-speaking tribe had lived along both rivers bearing the name.

Over time however, inter-tribal skirmishes, famine and colonial rule had resulted in something of a diaspora, with tribes often showing scant knowledge of, or respect for the colonial boundaries decided by Cecil John Rhodes and the Portuguese government.

The *VaLwena* (Lwena people) from around the Lwena river in Angola (now known as the Moxico province), crossed the Zambezi into Northern Rhodesia and after an inconclusive war against the Lunda, conducted with bows, arrows and spears, settled in the Lovale district.

In time, these Lwenas came to be known by some as *Balovale* (the Lovale people). It was at Balovale on the Zambezi river that the Northern Rhodesian government established a magistrate's court, post office and basic hospital and where another of the ubiquitous Brethren mission stations was established.

Igloo-shaped grass huts or mud and wattle houses with thatched roofs were built by the natives who also hollowed out canoes, shaped paddles and made crude clothing from skins or tenderised tree bark. The arrival of the treadle sewing machine, visible on the veranda of most trading stores, played a role in introducing clothes made from western fabrics.

There must, however, have been a certain amount of raw iron ore in the area. In some villages one would find a man smelting ore to produce what was probably really pig iron.

Effective bellows were made by the natives comprising a hand carved piece of wood with two chambers having two parallel funnels one protruding from each chamber. A soft hide diaphragm covered each chamber and a length of reed was gummed to the centre of each diaphragm enabling air to be forced through the funnels by pumping alternate reeds up and down. The double-nosed snout of the funnels would be positioned close to the hot coals to permit feeding air, thus maintaining a high temperature for smelting and forging.

Hoes, axes, spears, arrows and knives as well as other trinkets were made by native craftsman entirely from local material. The metal 'notes' of the *chisaji*, mentioned in another chapter, were produced this way. Here was a laudable and rare example of African enterprise.

Fishing was perhaps another example of Lwena enterprise. The Zambezi and its tributaries were always teeming with fish. Hand woven nets were used as described elsewhere and individuals would often cast a line using mostly the efficient barbed hook available at trading stores. Occasionally one saw a crude locally forged hook among the larger sizes. One motivated fisherman used to regularly ply his trade just below the Chavuma falls, in his own dug-out, selling his catch to local villagers and to the missionaries.

The Lwena-speaking people, had been in that area long enough for *Chavuma* to be the hereditary name of the local chieftainess.

Despite a chieftainess, the Lwena were a male-dominated society. Women worked the manioc fields, peeled and soaked the roots and carried loads of manioc, firewood or calabashes of water balanced on their heads. They raised the children, chased the goats away from food pots and even fished in the river.

Women were consequently more often in trouble from accidents or wild animals and were the main victims when the witch doctor called names. Native men enjoyed the sun and other pleasant pastimes though, as indicated, sometimes engaged in hunting, fishing and smelting.

Lwena means 'illegitimate child' so Lovale became more favoured as a name for the language and Balovale for the people. The Lunda tribe who laid claim to the Balovale district were of course unhappy about this.

The Logan family from Buffalo, N.Y. and two single missionary ladies Doris Mitchell and Gladys Richards from England were working at Chavuma when the Barnetts arrived. These busy people conducted all the Gospel and devotional services, a medical dispensary serving out-patients and providing some in-patient care, village preaching, educational teaching and administrative and maintenance work for this sizeable establishment with its growing number of out-schools.

The Barnett's Home at Chavuma

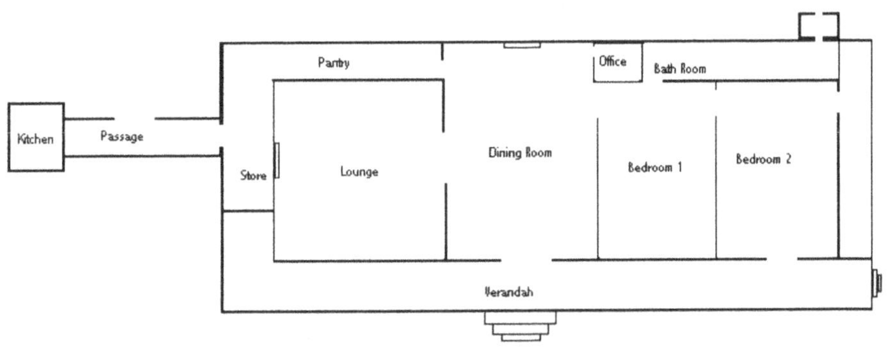

Plan of the Barnett's House at Chavuma

The thatched house built of poles, transverse saplings and mud, built earlier by Bert Sims, had been selected as the home for the new arrivals. More spacious than the corrugated metal house in Roodepoort, it had no water-borne sewage system, no ceilings, and only very basic amenities.

Home for the next 12 years, this house did not even have metal ant-proof coursing used in some houses to discourage termites who frequently voraciously ate out the inside of the poles leaving only the flimsy outer bark to keep the mud walls together and the roof up.

We had to share the house with moths, spiders, scorpions and other unwelcome visitors. These creatures loved to hide behind pictures on the wall and would crawl hastily to the next picture if disturbed. The thatched roof was another haven for a whole range of strange looking tropical insects - some of them designed to look more venomous than they were.

At night we used paraffin lanterns mostly of the hurricane variety and perhaps one or two beautifully designed brass lamps with glass shade and decorative knob for adjusting the wick.

Insects of varieties that only tropical Africa can boast were attracted by our lamps. Some exotic moths had concentric rings on the end of each wing making them appear sinisterly like Spitfires, the British World War II aircraft.

The moths in turn attracted predatory spiders such as the hairy and frightening tarantula. It was not unusual to see a tarantula crawl on to the supper table and speed across someone's dish in pursuit of an elusive six legged morsel.

One night, brushing her arm on her skirt, Mother was stung by a scorpion that had been clinging there. Most of us had this painful experience from time to time. An antidote recommended by some was to cut off the business end of the scorpion, wrap it in a morsel of food and swallow it.

Mosquito nets were compulsory. Suspended on the four bed-poles these nets were made to hang down at sunset and tucked in under the mattress. Movement during the night usually left an entrance for these insidious pests who in the morning light would congregate in the top four corners of the net. I have often clapped my hands together in just one corner, killing at least forty mosquitoes in one motion and leaving my palms stained with my own blood.
Refrigerators were unknown. A cabinet known as a "safe" with small gauge wire mesh on top and each side and its legs standing in a can of water, kept the homemade butter from melting into oil and the food safe from marauding ants and flies.
The staple food among the natives was a mush *(shima)* made of meal pounded from the manioc root, a South American tubular plant. We found this more than palatable when the flour was well sifted.

Mother's 'pot-boy' Hoxi, eager to learn a few English words, one day pointed out his discovery that English was similar to Lwena. As proof he offered the fact that while the VaLwena said *shima*, the English simply reversed it, saying "mushi".

Chavuma relied on the post office, magistrate's court and government hospital seventy-five kilometres south at Balovale. Apart from a native trading store selling truck to the villagers on the west bank of the river and another in Balovale, our nearest shops were located in Livingstone, a total of ten weeks' journey by barge. Canned foods and other supplies were ordered at intervals of several months.

Fresh foods such as meat, vegetables and tropical fruits like guavas, mangoes and bananas were purchased from local natives. While some fresh milk was available to make butter, powdered milk was the usual fare. Some oranges and bananas were grown on the hill. There were times when nutrition was problematical especially with small children.

Three sycamore trees planted by the Sims family in front of the house, were by now large and shady. The ground on the hill was very stony making gardening almost impossible. Some effort had been made to remove extremely large rocks to provide some depth of soil for a garden.

A discarded dug-out canoe was placed at one end of the area to provide a bed for flowers. Nearby stood a copper rain gauge.

Mother organised some labour to dig out more of the large rocks and to import topsoil to improve the gardening potential even further.

One day as the labourers lifted a particularly recalcitrant flat stone, an African cobra was disturbed. One of the workers approached intending to stone the reptile which reared up, puffed its hood and sent a streak of venom accurately into the man's eyes causing considerable pain. Mother's trusty medical book came in handy once again and she successfully treated the eyes, which had fortunately not taken very much of the venom.

In the rainy season Chavuma hill was brilliant with self-seeding Cosmos and Zinnias originally sown by the Sims family.

The white ant, a voracious termite, built its anthills everywhere. About 2 metres high, these conically shaped pinnacles dotted the countryside as far as the eye could see. Some shrubs and smaller plants, including a wild begonia, grew on mature ant hills. The clay produced by termites makes a material that is binding and not easily washed away by tropical storms.

One apparent luxury we did have. Employment in the Western sense was something rare indeed, but there were many natives, who with some guidance and training from the missionary could learn cooking, house cleaning, ironing and other chores.

Like most missionaries we were able to find, amongst the converted locals, a cook, pot-boy, house maid, two water-carriers and an ironer. The iron in which hot coals were placed was swung in the wind by hand to allow air, wafting through designed holes, to fan the coals when the temperature dropped.

As toddlers, my brother Walter and I had a nurse maid and when, in due course, our twin sisters arrived, the maid took over the new charges and we were taken on walks and kept out of danger by a faithful young native aide called Moni.

Mother employed and trained a sewing assistant who learned quickly and took pride in his skill.

Behind the house we had a carved wooden mortar about 100 cm in height in which peanuts or manioc were occasionally pounded using a smooth wooden pestle about 150cms in length.

A native woman hired for the task wood pound away usually singing as she worked. As often as not, she would be singing to her baby wrapped to her back. A common sight in the villages, was two native women pounding alternately into the same mortar with split-second timing and, usually each with a baby on her back.

Peanut oil from the pounding process was useful in cooking and a variety of other purposes. The pulp was given to the servants or used as feed for the chickens.

While these helpers were cheap enough, the horde had to be taught the rudiments of hygiene and sound domestic practises. They required supervision. Neither work ethic nor timekeeping have been a feature of labour in the continent. It was Bishop Tutu the South African Anglican Archbishop, who much later, charmingly referred to a tendency towards unpunctuality as "African time".

This help made it possible for missionaries, unused to the tropical conditions, to concentrate on mission work which would have suffered had they tried to perform all these domestic tasks themselves while fighting malaria, sunstroke and many undiagnosed diseases.

Paying the large staff only after they had attended the regular gospel services, was a sensible strategy in the achievement of the mission objective.

The great Zambezi river, known to the Lwena as the Yambezi, played an important role in our lives. Roads being scarce, the river was a vital waterway southwards for supplies in Livingstone and upstream to Angola and to the missionary school at Sakeji.

We had a veranda paved in local flat stone, abundant on the hill, with a magnificent view of the Zambezi river along 4 kilometres of its length. Visitors to Chavuma in recent times, whose impressions are recorded on the Internet, have described the panoramic viewof the mighty river in superlative terms.

Cataracts broke the surface of the river into contrasting runs of white water. At the north end of the view a couple of native villages could be seen on our side of the river. Across the river and up to the horizon the huts of more villages were visible through the trees. In the distance near the horizon could be seen grassy plains which provided grazing for herds of wild game and were in summer, flooded by a tributary of the Zambezi. Seasonally when the white egrets migrated northwards, large flocks flew in rough zigzag formation up stream, their white flecks on the blue water merging indistinguishable from the white water of the rapids.

The river supplied water to the mission, fetched from the Zambezi in calabashes or dried gourds *(musuhwa)* one fixed to each end of a palm pole with a rough rope made from the stripped bark of a tree and balanced on the shoulder.

These "drawers of water", like the Biblical sons of Ham, had to descend the steep hill on foot for about 2 kilometres to the river's edge, fill up and climb back with the precious liquid which had to be boiled for drinking. Tropical waters often contain dangers such as bilharzia and cholera. Canvas water bags bulging with boiled water, hung cooling by evaporation under the eaves of a covered passage way leading to the smoky kitchen with its wood burning stove. Like the drawers of water the "hewers of wood" too, were of the 'sons of Ham'.

The great river could be crossed by canoe or barge only at selected places where current, width and landing made this possible. One such crossing was directly below our house, so sitting on our veranda we could watch the hand paddled canoe edging its way slowly, first upstream before moving into the swift mainstream and being swept downstream while the paddler redoubled his effort to propel the boat beyond the main current and then upstream towards the opposite shore.

In order to facilitate attendance at meetings held on the station, co-missionary Wallace Logan initiated an effort to span the mighty river with a bridge. At that time the bridge at the Victoria Falls was the only bridge across the Zambezi from its source to its mouth in the Indian ocean.

Logan made it a project for the people who were urged to bring stout timbers and stones of a selected size to the east bank. His design was simple. The timber would be stacked to form a series of rectangular shaped stanchions with a corner facing upstream to reduce the area of resistance to the current. Each timber rectangle would be filled with stone. These island stanchions would be linked by timber walkways.

The project was launched at a well attended ceremony involving prayer, singing and dedication. There would be no pay. The valuable facility to the public and a boost to the mission work were going to be reward enough.

On one of the scheduled bridge-building occasions there were some native girls swimming up stream from the site, while others laid timber and threw in stone, when one girl became caught in the current and was swept swiftly down towards the work site. Logan rushed out to furthermost stanchion and reaching out as she passed screaming in terror, he barely grasped her hand pulling her to safety.

The idea was no doubt supportable in engineering theory and indeed, while public enthusiasm lasted, three such formations bravely reached out in line to a respectable distance from the shore. The theory that voluntary human effort would continue for the many months or years necessary for completion, did, however, not survive.

As more fully described in a later chapter, baptism among the Brethren was by the scripturally ordained method of immersion. The Zambezi served as a natural venue for baptism of converts. This had its risks and indeed a shelter of saplings or bamboo, bound with bark-rope, was usually built to protect the deep water side against crocodiles.

For Walter and me, the river was a fascinating place in which fish abounded and were easy to catch with a reed for rod, string for line and a bent pin for hook. Elsewhere, some of our boating escapades on small pools and lakes parallel to the river are described.

Missionaries were driven by a powerful sense of obedience to God. "Go ye into all the world and preach the Gospel and lo I am with you even unto the end of the age". No other explanation can be found for sacrificing career prospects and comfortable living and embracing health hazards and risking danger to life and limb without any guarantee of financial support.

Of course some missionaries enjoyed the glamour that came with such a courageous act and for some the "report back" meetings while on "furlough" were naturally ego boosting. As cine cameras and slides came into use some well-produced presentations aided the report-back task. Considering the genuine risks of disease and disaster however, they deserved any small bouquets thrown at them by the wide-eyed faithful back home.

American and Canadian missionaries were the best supported not only in so far as personal welfare, clothes and supplies were concerned, but equipment, or even a vehicle, came more readily from the USA than Britain. Perhaps the fact that the mission fields were all colonies of European countries, deglamourised the field in European eyes to some extent. Familiarity with natives may have bred contempt, clouding the heroic aura.

One tenuous theory would have us believe that America's well-known generosity towards its African missionaries is part of a guilt complex over historical slavery. Whatever the explanation, let it be said that Chavuma's American missionaries were always willing to share what they received, and showed the utmost kindness to all.

Beside the common task of evangelising, each missionary on the station would have specific responsibilities assigned usually according to training and experience, but often simply according to the needs of the moment. These included teaching, medical services, preaching, pastoral work, management, carpentry and building maintenance.

As indicated, according to Lwena custom, parents were renamed as father and mother of the eldest child. Missionaries readily accepted African names as a gesture of friendship and to avoid the often amusing attempts to pronounce English names.

Being the eldest I was given the name *Kapalu* and hence Fred became *SaKapalu* and Dorothy *NyaKapalu.* Walter was named *Kaumba,* my sisters Dorothy and Margaret were known as *Mulombwe* and *Kanyombo.*

Male missionaries were addressed as *Mwata* as a mark of respect and acknowledging, what in those times was accepted as, the proper seniority between natives and Europeans. Female whites were addressed as *Ndona,* a word adopted from Portuguese, probably because native culture did not need a word to elevate a woman unless she happened to be a chieftainess.

Wallace Logan was the senior missionary at Chavuma, a practical man much loved for his kind nature and wicked sense of humour. In an exception to the rule about taking the name of the eldest child, Logan was appropriately named *Kuunda* (man of peace).

His help and comradeship very quickly put my parents in a position to make an early contribution preaching, visiting and in practical work.

Wallace Logan initiated many improvements on the station. One of these, completed soon after arrival of the Barnetts, was a bell tower of timber, the platform of which housed a large church bell shipped from the United States of America and which swung on its cradle to call the villagers and the faithful to services.

A note on the back of a photograph in Mother's handwriting indicates that "it was built by Wallace and Fred". At the tower's inauguration, all the missionaries on the station at the time, clambered up the ladder-like steps to enjoy a picnic on the platform. That experience is one of my earliest memories.

In 1937 Wallace built a large meeting hall named the Tabernacle, a structure of thatch, timber and hand made brick, which could seat 4000. The design permitted warm air to escape while admitting sunlight. A conference of Brethren, 35 missionaries from the Beloved Strip and hundreds of natives, attended the opening.

Chavuma missionaries met weekly in one of their houses for the Sunday evening meal providing an opportunity for updating each other and for fellowship.

Gladys Richards and Doris Mitchell, at one time suspected that flour, sugar and other food was being stolen on the Sunday evenings during which they were eating at another house. A trap was set involving loyal house workers who wished to clear their names. They hid in the dark house with an electric torch. Their efforts were rewarded when a former cook entered and was identified.

While employed he had learned how to use these Western ingredients and was making biscuits in his village. It was then Mother recalled previously passing through his village and surprisingly, being offered some appetising looking biscuits obviously made from the stolen flour.

The Gladys, Doris and Mother, enjoyed a game of badminton tennis occasionally, on a reasonably good court.

On special occasions a convivial party would be held. There would of course be no liquor. Apart from the normal Brethren attitude towards alcohol, strong drink had to be condemned among the natives who brewed a toxic local beer with ingredients that frequently resulted in disastrous behaviour with fatal consequences.

About 3 years after the arrival of the Barnetts, a Canadian lady Irma Motter joined the mission team. She was a skilled teacher and also took on medical duties.

One of the native delicacies in season was the small caterpillar known in South Africa as the mopani worm. They were dug up from the soil, extracted from their cocoons and eaten cooked or raw.

Shortly after her arrival Irma, joined us in a visit to an out-school. After the gospel service and picnic lunch, most retired for a rest from the heat of the day. Even the acclimatized villagers seemed to be having the equivalent of a siesta that day.

Instead of resting, Miss Motter, eager to learn the ways of Africa, decided to taste some of these caterpillars. She sat with a small pot in which they had been cooked, picking off the wicked looking heads, popping the bodies into her mouth and throwing the heads over the veranda wall.

The Bell Tower

The Tabernacle

Irma enjoyed these tasty morsels and had discarded a good few dozens of caterpillar heads in this manner when to her horror a native elder who had, unknown to her, been dozing on the other side of the wall, awoke and stood up with his hair literally sprinkled with the heads of caterpillars. Realising the enormity of what she had done and having been warned against cultural insults, she uttered the only Lwena word she could muster in that moment. It was, rather irrelevantly: "Therefore!"

Shortly after that two more Canadians, George and Merle Butcher arrived. Both dedicated missionaries. George Butcher was a very practical man, so useful where infrastructure was concerned and his wife Merle was a talented singer and Hawaiian guitar player. Merle was also a calligraphist who labelled the dispensary medicine bottles in a style that would be the envy of most pharmacists.

I can still remember Merle Butcher singing: *"Into a tent where a Gypsy boy lay... tell it again... salvation's story repeat o'er and o'er".* The metal slider slurred the guitar chords in true Hawaiian fashion in accompaniment to, what we later came to recognise, as a country style singing voice.

During the Second World War Gladys Richards and Doris Mitchell were joined by Daisy Wareham from London. She had been unnerved by the blitz and was looking forward to some peace and quiet.

Unfortunately on the day she arrived at Chavuma, as part of the welcome, the natives fired off some musket muzzle-loaders of which the barrels had been stuffed with sisal fibres for additional effect. The loud bangs and accompanying ejection of the flaming sisal from the muskets were too reminiscent of the frightening sights and sounds of beleaguered London, which she had hoped to escape. Poor Daisy collapsed in hysterics.

Fortunately, though, this was a rare event as there was only a little gun-running from Angola at the time. Serious African addiction to firearms was only to emerge later with the *winds of change.*

Chavuma and Balovale missionaries naturally selected the local language to learn and for translation purposes. By doing so they unwittingly sided politically with the Lovale thereby annoying Lunda tribal remnants who laid claim to the area.

The Lunda tribe dominated territories to the north both in Angola and Northern Rhodesia, where many other Brethren stations were established; Kalene, Kavungu, Cazombo, Kalunda

My father *Mwata* SaKapalu and my mother *Ndona* NyaKapalu immediately set about becoming proficient in the Lwena language, to which Gavin Mowat had introduced them. In the meantime they spoke through an experienced missionary as translator.

Mother once told us the story of a new missionary using a local native translator to interpret an erudite sermon in which he sought to explain the exegetical distinction between *redemption, sanctification and edification.*

The translator who neither understood the differences himself nor knew any words in the vernacular to convey the concepts, resorted, unbeknown to the preacher, to using three native versions of "whatsisname". The primitive hearers were consequently subjected to a long and arduous treatise on the subtle differences between

the Lwena equivalents of "thingmebob", "thingmejig" and "watchamacallit".

As SaKapalu, the accomplished biblical student, had discovered when studying Zulu, the vocabulary of African tribes including Lwena, was not going to permit him to say much about "post millennial theory". Nor was "consummation of the ages", one of my father's choice expressions in English, likely to become a vogue phrase among the Lwena believers

Pronunciation was another trap since the phonetic spelling devised by the missionaries did not always permit distinction between minor shades of inflexion or accent. Hence there were instances of embarrassment in the use of the Lwena word spelled *tumbi*, which with an almost imperceptible change of emphasis, could mean either saviour or mouse. Undoubtedly those missionaries who never fully mastered the more subtle pronunciations, unwittingly spent many years confusing their hearers.

Fred was soon displaying his competence in the new missionary environment having quickly mastered the language and earned the respect and gratitude of many of the natives and of his fellow missionaries.

He also soon involved himself in practical work besides his penchant for preaching. An early 8mm black and white silent ciné film taken earlier by Wallace Logan and projected a few years later at a family evening, (just before a rather un-Brethren-like Charlie Chaplin cartoon), showed Fred Barnett supervising a team of native workers as they built roads linking missionary houses, church halls, dispensary, carpentry shop and other mission buildings. These paths largely comprised stone foundations with anthill clay for the surface.

Visiting villages remote from the mission was always a challenge involving excursions across hostile terrain. In a letter on 26th April 1932 my father describes some of the conditions.

"We set out on an itinerary to villages approachable to the Zambezi and journeyed by barge but on many occasions we walked 3 miles or more inland to villages sometimes through forest, other times across swamps, often in slimy mud".

Arriving back in camp a bath came before any refreshment. He describes one return journey after sunset with only a paraffin hurricane lamp to show the way:

"Our guide seemed to choose the worst paths.....tramping through slime composed of ox manure and stagnant water with persistent midgets getting

into our ears, noses and throats".

Father used a bicycle to get to out-schools and villages on the Chavuma side of the Zambezi.

Every week he would visit Sewe, a village out-school run by a faithful husband and wife team SaMbaulo and NyaMbaulo, where a service would be conducted.

Sometimes, as a 3 year old, he would take me on the bicycle luggage rack behind the saddle, an experience which I found frightening and uncomfortable. On the return journey as we freewheeled down the slope towards home I remember my father would push the spring lever of the bicycle bell to alert my mother that it was time to put the kettle on for a cup of tea.

I have a painful memory of one such journey when speeding down the slope from Chavuma hill, I slipped off the carrier and my leg became entangled between the rear wheel spokes and fork. This resulted in both of us being thrown off the bike and a tearful and grazed M.K. having his leg extricated from the wheel.

An addition to the family was expected. We trekked overland the seventy-five kilometres to Balovale, where a medical doctor was stationed, so that Mother could receive the necessary medical assistance.

Of course native babies were born daily in the rough conditions of the villages and, occasionally even along the footpath walking between villages. The death rate of babies was naturally very high, particularly before missionaries brought medicines and hygienic practices to Africa.

Walter and I were unaware of the expected domestic event and while our parents had other matters on their minds, we roamed around with native children enjoying the changed scenery Balovale had to offer the inquisitive minds with which most small boys seem to be endowed.

What made it more interesting was that Balovale was attacked by swarms of locusts at the time. Some days the cloud formed by the pests was so dense that the sun was dimmed, casting a moving shadow on the ground.

The arrival of locusts filled the natives with foreboding because both their meagre manioc crops, and to a lesser extent the natural vegetation from which they plucked sustenance, were at risk from these marauding pests.

I recall Walter and I amusing ourselves throwing stones up into the fast moving cloud of hoppers, hoping to knock a few down. Our native pals did indeed succeed in knocking down a few locusts, a sought-after delicacy to take home as relish for the pot and to enjoy with their shima.

I had been using a rough stick trying to prevent a fallen locust getting up and flying off when a sharp splinter pierced the thumb of my right hand so deeply that my father took me to the hospital where it was decided to administer an anaesthetic before attempting to remove the splinter. The chance of infection in the tropical environment was high. The unmistakable odour of chloroform terrifies me to this day.

In due course Walter and I had identical twin sisters Dorothy *(Mulombwe)* and Margaret *(Kanyombo)* born on 7th September 1932. Mother tied a ribbon around one of the four new ankles to make sure we got their identities right.

The addition to her responsibilities was a challenge in the primitive conditions.

The Christmas of 1932 is the first one I can remember. The party was an exciting affair at the Logan's house adorned with decorations and a Christmas tree, for which an indigenous shrub with bright red berries and glossy leaves had been used. Father played the role of Santa Claus, an unscriptural character, strictly speaking.

The faithful natives had dressed up as colourfully as they could and had paraded around the mission singing Carols in excellent harmony. The special lunch was, to me, a great feast including mugs of what the Logans called "Boston Cream", a soft drink whipped into a foam after adding a teaspoon of bicarbonate of soda.

The existence of Father Christmas had not been defended by the adults with the same fervour that biblically verified figures enjoyed. Indeed to many Brethren the festivity, including its tree, was largely a pagan idea and the selection of the date had been arbitrarily fixed anyway.

Perhaps it was the faint smile my parents had worn when discussing Father Christmas and the fact that my father had disappeared on some excuse, that the arrival of the man in a red suit with cotton wool beard didn't really fool me. "It's my Dad", I shouted wrecking the charade while a look of disillusionment appeared on the faces of some of the other Children of Chavuma.

To me, of more importance were the presents which much parental hinting and knowing comments from the older Logan twins Francis and Esther, had suggested might be forthcoming. Toys were a rarity that we could only dream of, yet some kind supporters had mailed gifts from Australia for the Barnetts from America for the Logans and from England for the single ladies.

From the dim memory of the occasion, one gift stands out. It was an attractively coloured tin of Bakers biscuits which, when unwrapped, revealed a thin metallic sheet sealing the contents and a gadget for cutting it open. Those delectably flavoured biscuits were a rare pleasure indeed at Chavuma.

My parents were now very busy missionaries who could be woken up at dead of night to provide medical care for a native mauled by a wild animal or have the busy schedule disrupted by the urgent need to travel to an out-school to sort out some trouble.

Now there were four small children. As the eldest, I was not yet 4 years,

Walter just 16 months younger and baby twins with special needs of their own.

Our parents never complained of the heavy work load or the responsibilities. They were, on the contrary, very happy to have the opportunities and the good health to serve. They trusted God for security and resources to meet all the challenges including raising the young family in difficult circumstances.

In a circular of 1 February 1933, Fred writes:

"A party of natives were journeying by canoe to Balovale, when a crocodile fiercely attacked the boat. A Christian was knocked out and with presence of mind swam well under the water as he had been warned by his elders. He managed to reach the shore minus a lump of flesh torn from his body. Another native overbalanced and fell into the water and was killed by the crocodile".

Recently coming across this item in Fred's news letter, I noted with some poignancy, that it was issued just five months prior to his own tragic accident.

5. Tragedy Strikes

At this point in my mother's life the symbolism of the river and its capricious nature becomes painfully tangible.

Fred Barnett was tragically drowned on 13th May 1933. He was crossing the Zambezi in a canoe just below the Chavuma falls on his way to investigate an opportunity to set up a venue for communicating the gospel message to people living in less accessible areas on the bank opposite the mission.

For this promising young life to be cut short only 3 years after heeding the call of God to Chavuma was a tragedy and a mystery, enough to shake the faith of the most pious.

The facts are related in the following article published on 15th May 1933 by Wallace F. Logan in "Sowing and Reaping" a missionary journal:

"Here in the jungle of Central Africa the whole country for miles in every direction is silenced in deep thought over the sudden home-call of our beloved friend Mr Fred Barnett.

Mr Fred Barnett and I started out on Saturday afternoon to see about a trader's place, which had been offered to us to be used as an outstation if possible.

When reaching the Zambezi river the native (SaMulesu - author) *took me across first and went back to get Mr Barnett. They did not go far when a wave came and filled the small native dugout. The boat capsized and Mr Barnett and the native caught hold of it. In a minute the swift current took the two at a tremendous speed down the river. The native having very little clothing managed to get to the shore, but brother Barnett with his boots and clothing soon sank*

Being on the far side of the river, I could not see very well and I ran along the bank following his helmet and something dark, which I though to be Mr Barnett floating down the river. I hoped to run along until he was out of the current and then swim to rescue him. Upon reaching the place where the current was slower I thought to loosen my unnecessary clothing but before doing so I climbed a tree that I might see clearly the object which I was following, but alas discovered it to be the boat that had capsized floating along.

As no natives were in sight I kept calling for help. In a few minutes I saw a native coming to me in a small dugout. I enquired if he had seen Mr Barnett and he said "No". I asked him to take me over quickly but his boat was so small that it turned over when we were about 3 feet from the bank. I then told him to return and hunt about for the body and call out for others. Later a larger boat was brought to take me across. By this time an hour had passed and no trace of Mr Barnett.

The natives gathered thickly and how I welcomed the arms of Christian brethren as they buoyed me up, for I was by now too weak to walk alone. All I could think of was poor Mrs Barnett with her four children. It was now getting dark. My wife (who was having a meeting in a nearby village) heard the news first and came hurriedly to meet me, but who would meet poor Mrs Barnett? Shortly after Mrs Barnett came along. Oh the marvels of God's grace. In this I have learned that no trial is too great for God. I could not talk to her, but the Lord must have told her, may the dear Lord reward.

She in quietness, before hundreds of heathen yielded to God's will.

Later we learned that a native who had witnessed the scene from the side of the river said Mr Barnett's hand rose above the water three times and then disappeared. From this description we judged that Mr Barnett was taken to glory quickly.

Two days have passed and natives have streamed in from all directions to show their love and sympathy to dear Mrs Barnett. At one time of the day there were so many that we had to suggest them entering at one door and walking past her and going out another door at the other end of the house. There were hundreds passed during this hour. She said "Oh! Please don't let them go away without the Gospel". At her request they marched from her room direct to the meeting house, where our native brethren told them of our Lord Jesus Christ.

Brother Barnett won a big place in the hearts of the headmen of the district and God had used him mightily among them.

The whole district is in tears. Today a heathen headman said to me: "The whole neighbourhood is sad and very few have eaten any food since we heard of the death of our friend and teacher of God."

It is the crowd passing through the house of Doris Mitchell and Gladys Richards, that I can remember clearly. Mother lay shocked on a couch in the living room. Wallace Logan, *(Mwata Kuunda)* also lay prostrate, distraught and in tears. The single missionaries took turns to look after the four of us children who as yet did not understand fully what had happened or why the adults were displaying such sadness and shock.

Other records of the event suggest that the canoe had been overturned by a crocodile and that my father's body had been taken by the reptile. While this was not proven conclusively, the Nile crocodile population in the Zambezi was extremely high, having not yet been decimated by hunters.

At most parts of the river, except in very fast moving currents such as at rapids, crocodiles were present in vast numbers. The fact that only the canoe and my father's helmet were recovered does support the generally accepted version. Indeed some maintained that in those infested waters it was hardly possible that a crocodile had not been involved.

Reflecting on the event in the years that followed, the mood of the great river again seemed to provide appropriate language to describe the darkness and gloom that threatened to overshadow the 'glorious' river. The relentless force and pressure of a formidable cataract was surely now my mother's experience. Deeper waters lay ahead and the course of the river was uncertain.

When an accident involves a man of God whose devotion and performance is meticulous to a fault, human reasoning is taxed beyond measure.

Does the Omnipotent sometimes choose not to prevent such a tragedy? Is there a randomness in the Almighty's dealing out of vicissitudes? The scriptural reference concerning God's letting the blessing of rain fall upon righteous and unrighteous alike, might suggest such random selection is a basic principle.

The universe itself, displaying, as it does, considerable order, seasonality and even predictability on the grand scale, is seemingly dependent upon a higher intelligence acknowledged and admired even by some scientists. Nevertheless the universe does appear, to the ordinary observer, to operate randomly most of the time.

Orthodox Christianity asks us to accept God's "permissive" will without question. Yet we are possessed of a reasoning faculty, presumably given by God, and indeed one to which he seems to appeal in scripture, for example, "Come let us reason together, saith the Lord " (Isa 1:18).

The Old Testament story of Job contains its own explanation of why that righteous man suffered. It was the Almighty's response to Satan's jibe that in Job's case, righteousness was no more than just a way to ensure God's favours of protection and prosperity.

However the intellectual riddle is not simply about why the faithful suffer while the lascivious often prosper. It extends to how such tragedy can be reconciled with promoting achievement of the main objective namely the extension of the gospel message and of the "kingdom of God"?

My sister Dorothy recalls being told some years later that Wallace Logan and Fred Barnett had prayed at the beginning of 1933 that 100 people would be saved that year. At the 13th May 1933 the record indicated 60 souls had been saved in the area of the Chavuma ministry. Before the fateful day was over another 40 indicated their wish to accept the faith.

Inherent in many of the answers given to the inquiring young mind as it developed, was the concept that the intellect grappling with the riddle is, after all, human and finite, and by definition, therefore, not capable of understanding such apparently contradictory and counterproductive events.

One interesting response from Brethren bible students was that some people work so closely with, and so devotedly for God that, in reward, he calls them to heaven earlier than others. The case of Enoch is cited. Enoch, the idea goes, walked often with God and the walks got steadily longer so that one day, after a particularly lengthy walk, God said something like: "Look my friend Enoch, we've been together so much and enjoyed so many walks, this time you might as well just stay here with me now".

Would it be irreverent to hope that Enoch did not leave behind a widow with four small children?

Dorothy Barnett 1937

6. Widow's Work

It was surely time to return home to Australia. The inhospitable, dangerous and dark Africa was no place stay with two babies and two infants all under the age of four. Had this brave widow not already done enough sterling work, set an amazing example of courage and commitment and, as the Christian world would admit, already led many souls to salvation?

"Well no," decided Dorothy Barnett. "I responded to a call to work as a missionary in my own right," she would explain to those who out of concern and sympathy urged her to go home. This included the Christian supporters in Australia who were unable to deter her from her purpose of continuing.

Mother's reaction to adversity was similar to that of Old Testament characters like Gideon, Moses or Daniel, about whom we were taught so much. Their obedience gave them enough confidence to hold God to his undertakings. In similar circumstances, Moses might have said: "Well God you sent me to Bible Institute and called me out here. I obeyed and came to do the job, so now its up to you".

Some pertinent memories recalled by Eleanor Sims (born Logan) who with her brothers and sisters grew up alongside our family at Chavuma, are recorded in her own words:

"We have often used your mother as a wonderful example of one who was totally committed to her Lord and a godly, devoted mother to her four children. How many missionaries today would have packed their bags and returned from the mission field to go back home when a loved life-partner was so suddenly and tragically taken away! But so devoted to her Lord was your mother that her continuing on was such a testimony to those among whom she worked who through fear of death would have fled from the village assuredly believing that the "evil spirits" ("midzimu") were against her and would do even more harm to her. The heathen custom was to burn down the house and flee to a new location."

"Your mom was not without moments of sorrow and loneliness overcoming her. Once when sitting next to her at an evening meeting in the village around a fire I noticed tears dropping from her eyes, but not wanting to distract from the Gospel being preached, she bravely shielded her eyes. Yes, she was always more concerned for the need of others that she would not be a hindrance to them".

Of great comfort to my mother was the hymn "Like a River Glorious" which describes the promise of God's peace.

Sitting at the organ she would sing of that peace:

"perfect yet it floweth fuller every day,
perfect yet it groweth deeper all the way"

She deserved and experienced a tranquillity that was not normal in human terms.

As Eleanor has pointed out, there were, of course, moments when she was tearful, feeling the loneliness, missing Fred, facing a huge task.

She wrote on 5th December 1933:

"...the children - well I just praise the Lord for them day by day. They have been and are such a blessing. Sweet smiles and baby ways have been used many times to take my mind off my sorrow. Gavin the eldest saw me weeping over a letter received from a close friend, soon after dear Fred's home-call, and wanted to know why.

I explained, so he replied: 'But Mummy, Daddy has gone to be with Jesus and I am getting a big boy, I will take care of you'. He will be five years old on New Year's day, bless his heart".

In telling me this story as an older boy, Mother had mentioned that I had used the Lwena word *lama* (take care of). It was an emotional moment finding this record in Mother's letter sixty eight years later.

Thirty six years after the event, an industrial psychologist consulting in career aptitudes, dragged the incident out of me and triumphantly seized upon the story as proof that my aptitudes lay in the direction of "line" rather than "staff" management.

As time passed there were moments when it was I who needed some line management treatment. Mother told me that I had soon begun testing the boundaries of discipline, a rather natural process especially when the male parent is no longer present. She had to cope with these challenges of a single parent and met them firmly yet understandingly.

Being the eldest, Mother naturally confided in me to an extent unusual for my age. This gave me an early insight into the otherwise sacrosanct territory of adults.

A typical day in the life of Nyakapalu could find her dealing with responsibilities spanning a very wide range including preaching, teaching, medical care, travelling, bringing up a family and a host of unexpected activities.

While the communication of the good news is the principle objective of Christian missionary work, the responsibility was discharged in ways suited to the audience and occasion.

Mother's preaching could include leading a bible study in a reasonably comfortable room but equally it might take the form of a service in a primitive village surrounded by inquisitive natives seated on the ground. Being out in the open chickens, sheep and goats oblivious of the solemnity of the meeting, roamed around all the while pecking or nibbling for sustenance, and scrawny tykes lay still in the heat, their ears occasionally flicking off a persistent fly.

The portable Estey organ assembled and its pedals pumping the bellows, would bring wonderment and delight to the villagers many of whom would never have seen such a device or heard such magical harmony. In a letter of 28th April 1932, my father had mentioned the effectiveness of the portable organ played by Mother when they toured remote villages.

Mother's talent for music and her true soprano voice leading the singing would soon have the 'congregation' lustily singing a hymn they had never heard before.

Having gained their attention to a degree rarely managed in a cathedral, the hearers would then be treated to the message of salvation attainable merely by faith.

One such service was interrupted when curiosity got the better of a man who crawled towards the organ and gazed up at the two bellows being pedalled up and down alternately. When Mother noticed him she paused at the end of the next verse and asked him what he was doing. He answered that he was trying to see the man in the box who was singing so nicely.

Of course, during the short furlough in Melbourne she engaged in another form of preaching. Here the objective was largely a report back to supporters. Unbelievers were also welcome so that they might hear the gospel preached by someone who was clearly much more than a mere theorist on the subject.

Being strictly biblical in their practices, the Brethren generally sided with the Apostle Paul on the question of women's audible participation in the church, though women addressing women was acceptable.

After one report back occasion during Mother's furlough, a 'sister' asked rather disapprovingly: "do you speak to men?"

Mother answered in the affirmative pointing out that in many situations in the African mission field there was not a man within several days journey who was capable of or willing to do the preaching, and asked whether in those circumstances the lost were to be denied salvation on the basis of a legalistic interpretation of scripture.

Mother used to explain Paul's exhortation that women keep silent in the church, as being, quite possibly, an ad hoc suggestion to deal with a local cultural tendency of ladies to chat and gossip during a service rather than a universal doctrine which applied mindlessly, could actually hinder the work.

Reflecting, in later years, on my mother's sensible interpretation I have often imagined the apostle, hearing the discussion and being thoroughly amused. From his vantage point, he would supposedly be able to see the men attending the service dressed only in loin cloths made of peeled and tenderised bark, listening with the vacant expressions of the illiterate and seated in polite deference to the white (female) speaker. Painting such ridiculous scenarios are often the best antidote for those who would focus more on raising dogmatic obstacles than offering a helping hand in circumstances where the practicalities are not otherwise conducive.

Quoting Eleanor again:

"Another lovely memory of your mother was when the twins were younger and had both come down with measles. This took place while trekking in the villages, accompanying our parents, spreading the Gospel. With the distress of a glaring sun on the tent where the twins were and knowing eyes needed to be shielded from extra brightness and heat when suffering from measles and the further discouragement of well-meaning Africans gathering around crying loudly to "comfort" her, what did she do? Her selflessness in thinking of their great need of being without a Saviour caused her to sit down and translate the words of "Turn your eyes upon Jesus", into Luvale. Having done that she quietened the crowd and sat down and taught them how to sing this lovely chorus in their own language, Luvale. After that many learned that that was the chorus to be sung when in deep distress".

Walter, who also remembers the occasion 68 years ago, recently sat down and tried to recall the Lwena words Mother had written with such creative talent and so quickly. His effort was nearly Word-perfect. Eleanor confirmed that the Lwena Hymn Book reads:

Tumutalenu Yesu; tutale kumeso enyi:

Tuvulyame vyuma vyahamavu, nakuzanga vyamwilu kaha.

While generally, the inhabitants were willing to sit and listen to what the amazing white preacher had to say, there was a measure of opposition behind the scenes. This arose probably from the fact that missionaries preached against witchcraft, ancestral worship and some of the more gruesome cultural and superstitious practices. This is examined more fully in a later chapter.

One of the techniques used to intimidate or frighten women, children and any doubters, into respect for the witchdoctor was to parade the *mukishi.* This was a dervish figure wearing a fearsome, hand-carved wooden mask and decorative cloak intended to disguise his identity.

Mukishi were supposed to have risen from the dead and were often used at ceremonial occasions such as village dances. Even those who were not deceived by the disguise often harboured a superstitious fear of forces represented by the ritualistic charade.

My sister Dorothy recalls an occasion when accompanying Mother on a visit to villages, there was an apparently deliberate attempt to obstruct the Christian message by introducing two menacing *mukishi.* The villagers showed intimidation and some ran away.

Mother however calmly stood up and spoke, asking the mukishi to remove their masks so that the villagers could see this was a deceitful masquerade. My sister recalls that "many were saved" on that occasion.

Preaching was of course not confined to meetings for that purpose.

Mother never lost any opportunity to raise the critical issue of salvation whether it was informally greeting someone she met while walking, attending to wounds of someone attacked by a wild animal or paying wages to a servant for the day's work.

Life expectancy has always been abnormally low and still-birth rates high in tropical Africa, due to conditions which harbour mosquitoes, wild animals and disease. Lack of hygiene and primitive methods of ridding the village of unwanted people, also contributed to the statistics.

Revolting practices and conditions helped to limit an irresponsible population growth to levels which were viable in the face of little or no agricultural activities and the available food garnered from forest and plain. Feeding families has been traditionally left to women who laboured ineffectively in planting, harvesting, peeling, drying and pounding into a flour, the staple diet of manioc.

Locusts and famine kept the food supply erratic and unpredictable and even the eating of locusts redressed this situation only in a minuscule measure of poetic justice. Reproduction however was predictable, unintelligent and uncontrolled.

The truly enormous work done by missionaries through medicine, care and hygiene in tropical Africa as well, of course, as the condemnation of cruelty and murder, naturally tended to actually extend life expectancy. Ironically this resulted in a side effect that was anything but a blessing. Population growth, previously balanced by a combination of natural hazards and human savagery, had become more unchecked

Historically, surges in local populations have led to fighting for territory, space and water resources. Ethnic or tribal division inevitably marked the opposing sides. The resultant war combined with natural and cultural hazards, usually reduced populations to a more viable level and so a certain amount of coexistence was crudely restored.

It has to be said that modern times in Africa have not been very different in this respect and the end of the colonial era has seen a clear reversion to this cycle. The over-population and ethnic strife have now been exacerbated by the tide of HIV Aids fanning further, what is today described by the outside world as, 'Afro pessimism'.

Christian missionaries of course had a number of good reasons to provide medical treatment despite hostile conditions. There is ample Biblical support for showing care and dispensing healing to the sick and the fact that much of the biblical healing is recorded as miraculous, did not discourage the missionaries' use of medicine, suitably ranked in importance after the saving of souls, of course.

Much of the scientific medical treatment by dedicated missionaries had such a dramatically positive effect on neglected or mistreated cases, that many patients and onlookers were more than ready to believe in miracles.

Medical treatment therefore had positive consequences in the form of conversions.

Furthermore missionary kindness and tenderness shown among savage communities, provided excellent models of the changed behaviour Christianity could potentially bring.

Of course missionary medical resources were limited and they often faced opposition from diviners and witchdoctors. By and large however missionaries were seen as being in touch with the God of whom they spoke and who, in medical matters, displayed
little awe either for the ways of the ancestors or their after-life influence upon current events.

The missionary was therefore the logical person to whom all problems would be referred, especially where the witchdoctor had failed. An attraction was that the solution was always free of charge, except for having to listen to a possible sermon.

Like a refreshing stream that salves the injuries and quenches the thirst of those who come down to the waters edge, my mother's life included treating and nursing as the need arose.

She was confronted one day on the covered but otherwise open passage to the kitchen, where, on occasion, an iguana or snake would pay us a visit. Canvas water bottles hung swinging in the breeze, cooling our boiled Zambezi drinking water by evaporation. A man who's right arm seemed to be hanging lower than his left and obviously in great pain appealed to her for help.

Mother moved the arm around a bit to detect any break. Finding none, she went to fetch her thick medical book. Eventually she nodded authoritatively, raising the poor man's hope, all the while wondering whether she could really help in this situation.

"I think you have a dislocated shoulder" she said in English. The patient to whom the language was Greek seemed as enlightened as the 8 year old bystander that I was. Mother turned a few pages of the omniscient tome. The word "dislocated" like so many English words had no real equivalent in Lwena.

"Your arm is broken" she explained. He seemed well aware of that. "It has come out of its place in your shoulder", she explained further. That too, he was entirely prepared to believe.

Mother ordered the patient to sit with his back against the wall. She read a few more sentences from the book, mustered her courage and focusing on her duty with that look of fortitude she often wore when she felt inadequate, raised her leg in an un-ladylike stance and placed her boot firmly on the man's chest near the shoulder pushing his back against the wall. She then took hold of his hanging arm and, without warning, jerked it towards her with as much force as she could manage, releasing it to spring back into the socket.

The patient's yelling filled the air. Using Lwena words, many of which would never be appropriate for a missionary to translate, he addressed his mama and all his other ancestors.

But soon, finding himself still alive, the patient looked down at his arm, no longer dangling ineptly. Wearing a look of amazement, he walked off unsteadily, marvelling at the magic of the *chindele,* a Lovale name for white people meaning literally, white devil.

Feeling a little exhausted but triumphant, Mother carefully put away the medical book with its practical tips, for the next occasion and put the kettle on the cast iron Esse stove, for the cup of tea she so loved.

Chavuma operated a dispensary which served mainly outpatients suffering from snake bite, undiagnosed sickness or the results of the witchdoctor's attentions. There was limited accommodation for in-patients. Chavuma had no resident doctor.

Though not a trained nurse, Mother, whom it will be remembered, nursed her terminally ill aunt for over a year, helped in general nursing and treatment services of the mission. She also did some diagnostic work including the use of a microscope in identifying a particular culprit such as the *ankylostoma* or hookworm. Always keen that we should be learning, Mother showed us the parasite with its distinctive hook visible under the microscope.

In a Chavuma annual report for 1934 published by the Australian Missionary Tidings, Mother wrote:

"During the year we have been successful in treating various diseases such as hookworm, pneumonia, typhoid, measles..."

Malaria and blackwater fever were rife. Missionaries took quinine tablets daily to reduce the chances of these debilitating diseases. Unfortunately quinine is now known to affect hearing. A ringing sound in one's ears after the daily dose, was a common symptom. In later years hearing deterioration has become evident in my case and that of my siblings, together with many other M.K.'s from tropical Africa.

One of the common medical problems in the villages was severe burns occasioned by inhaling a local potent tobacco and falling in a stupor into the wood fire burning inside the hut. Since huts always had grass thatched roofs and often the entire hut was made of grass thatch in an igloo shape, fire hazard was indeed considerable and many fatal cases resulted. Mother wrote of such a case in a letter dated 3rd March 1934 in which, having naturally attended to the burns, she appealed for prayer concerning the patient's spiritual welfare.

In a letter of 13th April 1935, Mother wrote: *"A little girl was brought to the hill badly mauled by a hyena...."*

The sleeping girl had been pulled out of her hut by a hyena. The entrance to the hut had merely a bamboo woven door propped up against it. The hyena had been chased off by yelling villagers brandishing flaming sticks pulled from the embers of the village fire. Having lost blood and in pain she was carried to the river and ferried across in a dug-out. By the time she had been carried up the steep hill to the mission, she was in a seriously weakened state. Fortunately the treatment given was successful and she recovered, albeit with lasting scars.

There were no regular working hours for missionaries. Mother was wakened many times at dead of night to attend to injuries or serious illness. While some medicines were kept at the house, these occurrences usually meant braving the hazards of the African night and a walk in the dark carrying a kerosene wick lamp up the slope to the dispensary. There the patient mauled by a wild animal or wounded in a fight and carried up the hill by relatives would receive whatever treatment she could give. Often the medical condition had been aggravated by witchdoctor treatment which frequently involved stanching an already septic wound with a clod of clay mixed with herbs or leaves.

Once late at night Mother had to attend to a native woman who had been grabbed by a crocodile while fishing in the Zambezi. The woman had been lucky to escape as this reptile has a distinct advantage once its victim is in the water. The patient was severely shocked and her limbs mauled, exposing the bone. The kind but very basic treatment Chavuma was able to provide enabled the patient to avoid an amputation. Her recovery was slow and she was severely crippled for life.

Native women often fished while swimming. They used a woven basket with an oval shaped opening, to sweep the water, allowing minnows and fingerlings to swim into the basket and be scooped up on to the beach. These small fish were dried in the sun and made a strong savoury relish to eat with *shima.*

On another occasion just before retiring to sleep I heard a knock on the door and went with my mother to open up. A native woman carrying her very ill baby came in. Mother asked a few questions ascertaining that the witchdoctor had administered some treatment over a few days. She took the baby which died almost immediately in her arms. The native mother wailed in a loud, high pitched voice, "the missionary has killed my baby!"

Most of the mission stations had small round thatched huts built to accommodate aged native women who had been ejected from their villages.

Such ejection was a part of the native tradition in which the culture appeared to harness nature in keeping down the population the level of which was exacerbated by irresponsible family sizes.

Women who were no longer able to grapple with the challenge of food supply were especially vulnerable.

When a calamity such as a lightning strike burnt down a house or killed a villager, the witchdoctor would be consulted to identify the villager who, it was held, had connived with the evil spirits to bring about the disaster or had angered the ancestors in some way. Diviners were usually smart people who could see that a non-productive villager and one who might soon suffer the perils of old age would be the logical one to be selected for blame and whose departure would reduce pressure on the village economy. The diviner could usually also be suborned by anyone with a grudge.

One of the more interesting methods used to identify or name the culprit, is more appropriately described in the chapter on superstition. As soon as the villager with the evil spirits had been identified by the diviner, no time was wasted in either stoning the culprit to death or ejecting her from the village to starve or be killed by those carnivores who, like the victim, were too old to hunt for food in the usual way.

The Mission station was the only refuge and the missionaries received no congratulation for this gesture. On the contrary the divining profession perceived this as interference and opposition.

Ironically by almost every action whether by punishing murder or opposing the more outrageous practices of a savage African culture, white people were engineering a longer life expectancy for natives despite the fact that the missionary purpose and message were primarily concerned with the life hereafter.

Quite frequently when travelling through villages we would come across a man sitting with his bare back covered in protruding cones giving a porcupine effect. These were patients of the witchdoctor who had diagnosed the patient's problem as bad blood. Not always a bad guess.

The cure was to have the blood sucked out of the patient. The instrument was a mass of small conically shaped gourds or even the horns of a goat or small antelope. At the sharp end, a small hole was pierced. On the patient's back a number of cuts were made with a locally made un-sterilised knife. A cone was placed over the bleeding wound and the indigenous physician would suck the pierced end of the cone to draw blood, quickly placing a small piece of bees wax over the hole to seal the vacuum created by the sucking.

The cone would stay in place, slowly filling with blood. The poor man would have to sit still for up to a day while his 'bad' blood was drawn.

Leeches, plentiful in tropical rivers, would have been a more effective method, as physicians in Europe knew a century or so before. Of course the European doctors (or leeches as they were known at one time) did not, as far as I know, use the extracted blood for magic purposes as is still the case in many parts of Africa today.

Leprosy was common among the natives in those days. It is largely thanks to missionaries supported by the organisation then known as the Mission to Lepers that the disease is far less prevalent today.

Mother used to cycle to villages where known lepers lived in dire poverty and unsightly suffering. A message of hope for the after-life would be delivered and Mother would lead the singing of hymns with her appealing soprano voice and the strumming of her guitar. Many of these stricken people were converted and appreciated the kindness and medical attention they received.

The medical programme included some dental work too.

The natives had their own teeth cleaning practices. One was to use a small stick chopped from a selected bush and on which the bark was retained. One end of the stick was pressed against the teeth fraying the wood strands into what almost became a brush. In the process the sap of the twig oozed out and presumably reinforced the cleansing effect.

A much more primitive method also prevailed. Some readers may have noticed the many natives in central Africa with teeth that have been shaped to a point leaving a wide gap between each tooth and giving a saw-tooth effect.

This was achieved by actually taking a sharp knife and, using a mallet, chipping each tooth into that pointed shape. Some filing was then done to avoid rough edges. The usual explanation given was that it avoided the foul taste in the mouth on waking up in the morning. I remember one informative character saying that during sleep, one's teeth sneaked out and ate all sorts of things, some of which are rotten and inedible.
The 'morning-after' oral state was, by all accounts, an after-taste of an adventurous night out by one's teeth. How knocking them into a saw tooth pattern solved the problem was not clear unless it was that the wider spaces between teeth prevented bits of food sticking.

This 'night-out' explanation may have been a rationalisation of a custom begun in bygone eons, but which now served to make adults more attractive to the opposite sex.

I recently came across an internet snippet reading:

"rumour has it that there is a tribe in the Chavuma district that still sharpen their teeth with files, which was banned by the government in the 60's. But their ancestral traditions are very strong in these remote areas."

Occasionally a villager would arrive with severe toothache, a malaise common to all species irrespective of the decorative shape of their teeth.

At Chavuma mission any available missionary would extract the offending molar using an all-purpose forceps. Wallace Logan used to pull teeth outside his office, where appropriately a large hippo skull stood with mouth wide open revealing gigantic molars as a role model of what was required of the patient. The message seemed to be: "If you think you have pain, imagine how this guy suffered with teeth that size!"

Placing on record that my mother was a skilled and effective teacher truly understates how resourcefully she tackled the challenges in that side of her work.

It may be worth a moment's pause to consider the realities.

A primitive language, and still worse, one that is unwritten, is a serious handicap, in the formation of ideas and transfer of knowledge.

Unless a language contains a word for a concept, it is almost impossible for the thought or idea to be conceived, let alone conveyed. Thus primitive languages without even an alphabet, seem destined to retard learning other than through the spoken word or by real experience.

Even where basic words are used to describe an experience or ailment, such words are frequently steeped in culture or idiom so that, for example, an event may be described in language which assumes a superstitious cause attributing it even to evil spirits. In these circumstances exactitude and scientific basis are usually victims.

Three centuries after the first Europeans settled on the southern part of the continent, most indigenous languages, despite having absorbed a host of words from English, Portuguese and French, are still not used successfully in education, law or commerce for that matter. The inability of the languages to express more than a basic range of ideas, must surely have had its effect upon the very conceptualisation of new ideas. No wonder that in the twenty first century, democratic South Africa makes no apology for using English for most communication of any practical or legal significance, while making much ado about showing some politically correct respect for the ten, or so, indigenous languages and 25 dialects.

A statistical correlation between inadequate language and apparent levels of intelligence is not surprising. However, which of these is cause and which effect, is not popular as a debating subject.

It has become politically incorrect to attribute lower performance and slow learning ability to anything other than a conspiracy of poverty on the part of the colonial masters.

Apart from designs in beads, the colourful patterns on houses of some tribes and the well-known bushman paintings, Africans seem to have had no form of written communication at all. Egypt, where hieroglyphics was used centuries ago as every schoolboy knows is, of course, on the African continent.

In practical terms at least, missionaries of the 19th and 20th centuries had no way of translating and committing the Bible to writing in indigenous languages until a formal spelling system had been developed, which phonetically conveyed the sounds and, where possible, inflexions used in speech.

Pioneer missionaries and colonial officials provided a valuable service without which neither would have been able to carry out their important work.

Little recognition has been given to the role played in developing Africa, by the codification of native languages. Today it is politically correct, not only to deny that the colonial era produced any benefits at all, but also to maintain that all Africa's ills can be attributed to the greedy imperialist.

In addition to the Bible, the development of written form permitted the teaching of hymns and widened the distribution of the gospel through tracts. This had of course been the purpose of my father's printing work in

South Africa and as recorded, Gavin Mowat, founder of Chavuma mission was busy translating the Bible into Lwena at the time the Barnetts left South Africa for the interior.

However for the developed written form to be any use, reading had first to be taught to the illiterate. Missionaries who did not see general education as their primary responsibility had, often to engage in teaching reading and writing. In most mission schools arithmetic was also taught though its uses were perhaps seen as more material than spiritual.

Message in Song

Mother was an excellent teacher able to make the class experience interesting and also capable of devising some insightful ways of conveying understanding of mathematical concepts thus avoiding the blind alley of parroting.

She did use rote learning where it served a good purpose such as getting multiplication tables into one's head, but tried hard to ensure cognition too.

Perhaps the Brethren disapproval of "vain repetition" in which religious catechisms are repeated at length without necessarily changing behaviour or real belief, triggered off Mother's approach of learning with understanding.

She frequently drew simple animal or fruit figures on the blackboard as an aid to addition and subtraction. A very simple yet effective technique she personally developed, was to reverse the process after each arithmetic transaction. She realised the merit of recognising, for example, that subtraction is the reverse of addition. To achieve this she would write:

$3 + 2 = 5$, followed immediately by:

$5 - 2 = 3$.

The equations were illustrated with chalk-drawn coloured tomatoes or bananas.

Slates rather than paper, were used for writing exercises.
Some of the local mission-taught native adults were smart enough to assist in teaching. One of these was Maseka, a church elder and leader of a nearby out-school. In mission terms he was a highly respected senior Christian. Physically he was extremely short, a modern Zachaeus.

One day Gladys Richards, one of the more formidable single missionaries at Chavuma, came upon a class of children in an uproar. She singled out as the ringleader, a sturdy looking activist in the thick of the melee and grabbed him by the scruff of his neck. It turned out to be Maseka. Far from being the culprit, he had been trying to quell the insurrection.

Mother found time to teach singing to choirs and quartets. Natives were for the most part musical and easily adapted their own natural minor harmonic scale to the major scale of most Western music.

Those taught by Mother or used to singing in church, easily discarded their preference for dissonant chords, singing the harmony as instructed.

However "raw" villagers, as we rather impolitely referred to the untutored, would pick up the melody of a new hymn very quickly but harmonise with minor chords even
where Mother's guitar stridently indicated a major.

A feature of this indigenous harmony was the closing chord, which would invariably change the final major tonic chord common in Western music into a minor. This was achieved by singers of the bass part sounding out the one note of the final chord which turns a major into a minor. They seemed to gather enthusiasm for that last triumphant chord belting it out in a crescendo as a minor, just when our Western ears were expecting the major.

When Walter and I wanted to raise a laugh while singing at home or in missionary company, we would imitate this tendency to end the last line on a minor, causing deliberate consternation.

It has been interesting, some 77 years later, to come into possession of a letter my father wrote on 6th June 1926 while still in South Africa, to Dr C. H. Nash, principal of the Melbourne Bible Institute, stating:

"The natives have a peculiar way of singing which is all their own; singing without an accompaniment, they fall into natural parts which harmonise well in some hymns and creates frightful discord in others."

Most readers will be familiar with the hand held instrument sold to tourists and consisting of a carved and decorated wood base with eight metal bars of different length and thickness, which when snapped downwards with the finger, emit a musical note. It sometimes had a calabash attached behind to enhance resonance. The metal bars whose length and size determined the exact note required, would often have a piece of wax fixed to the broad front end which seemed to assist in producing the exact tone wanted.

Plucking each metal bar in sequence, produced the minor scale to which I refer. Unlike most Western instruments which allow selection of major or minor chords, and indeed other harmonic variations, this instrument like many others in Lovaleland, was limited to one minor key. The instrument was known as the *chisaji* amongst the Lwena, but so also were other musical instruments like the sarimba *(xylophone)* which also had a minor sequence in the scale.

Mother's teaching ability was recognised beyond Chavuma. She was asked to teach temporarily at the missionary school, Sakeji about which we have more to say in another chapter. At Sakeji, this self-taught intrepid lady, performed as one among fully trained equals.

Some keen adult students at Chavuma expressed a wish to learn English. I recall one who had become a teacher at the mission school and displayed some confident attitudes which missionaries found rare among his tribe. He was even thought of as slightly 'cocky' especially since requesting he be taught English. The Chavuma missionaries debated the wisdom of such a move. I recall hearing one missionary say something like "We don't want him getting above his station". This reference was deciphered for me by my mother when I queried its meaning. It represents an extraordinary attitude but, I suppose, one which was not unusual in the colonial era.

On reflection I believe the main hesitation arose from missionary priorities. If the gospel could be successfully propagated in the vernacular, then missionaries had plenty of work to do without becoming involved in broader educational problems which were not their prime responsibility.

Everyone of the servants referred to had to be taught their function except perhaps the water-boy.

Mother taught one young man how to operate the old treadle sewing machine. He was an intelligent fellow and loved the sound of the machine as it raced across the fabric working its magic with thread, bobbin, shuttlecock and needle. Soon he was doing quality work and saved Mother having to find time for running repairs on our clothes.

Learning such a skill was potentially useful since, apart from the missionary's needs, most trading stores had someone sitting at a similar machine on the veranda making simple clothing from the material sold.

Mother's teaching prowess extended to her own children. With the only white school two weeks journey away through punishing and dangerous territory, the four of us learned the three R's from our mother's knee. We were able to read and write confidently before we ever attended formal school.

At the outbreak of the Second World War in1939, we had been evacuated from Sakeji school as described more fully elsewhere. During the ensuing 12 month period at Chavuma, Mother ably substituted as teacher in the numerate and literary subjects and obtained what books she needed to keep her children's learning process alive.

I have since thought on those days and wondered where my mother, trained as a dressmaker, could have learned about past participles, mixed metaphors and split infinitives.

Excellence in one's work requires above average effort even where the infrastructure is conducive to raising a family and the after-hours environment is comfortable. Where working hours have no distinct starting and finishing times, the climate is irritating and the human material indifferent, achievement of excellence is of course quite extraordinary.

Water was plentiful in the mighty Zambezi that flowed two kilometres below Chavuma hill. But as described, this most basic requirement had to be carried tortuously, in gourds or calabashes lashed to a pole.

To avoid Bilharzia and other tropical diseases, the water had to be boiled before use. Drinking water was cooled by evaporation in canvas bags suspended from the rafters, there being no means of refrigeration.

Zambezi water was poured from the calabashes into a galvanised tank of about 850 litres built into an outside fireplace where it was heated by a wood fire. Piping from the tank led to a rugged zinc bath in what we liked to call the bathroom. Bath time clearly needed a little pre-planning. This arrangement was a lot more sophisticated than the bucket heating and bucket carrying that existed when the Barnetts first arrived at Chavuma.

In later years Wallace Logan, ever the progressive engineer, installed a diesel pump and piping which permitted Zambezi water to reach the mission hill more efficiently, though maintenance emerged as a new problem. The pressure on the pipe of a column of water pumped up to about 200 metres frequently resulted in repairing leaking joints. Supplies of diesel fuel were problematical being 10 weeks journey away at Livingstone. Wallace Logan experimented fairly successfully mixing diesel oil with locally grown linseed oil extracted from cotyledons of the flax plant.

Logan even built a swimming pool on the hill which provided a wonderful boon and a way to fight off the searing tropical heat.

With no water borne-sewage and a hard stony ground, toilets operated on the bucket system. Care in hygiene was a constant challenge in the tropical climate.

I have already described Mother's "safe" for protecting foods against both heat and ants.

Some foods were obtainable from the natives who were encouraged by the missionaries to produce milk, meat and some vegetables. The principle staple diet of the natives and to a large extent the Barnetts, was a paste made of flour derived from the manioc root.

In the 1500's the Portuguese first encountered manioc or cassava, the staple diet of the Indians in South America. It may have been introduced to Africa by the Portuguese colonialists.

Manioc is a carbohydrate-rich food that is easy to propagate but difficult to process, at least for the bitter variety, which is poisonous when raw. It is astonishing that the Indians ever discovered these tubers to be edible at all.

To be detoxified, tubers have to be soaked in water, peeled and grated and the pulp compressed to express the poisonous juice.

Lwena natives usually soaked the tubers at the river's edge or in wells, pounded the peeled roots and sun-parched the pulp on mats raised on stilts. The pulp was then removed, washed and roasted, rendering it safe to eat. The product was a coarse meal or flour. The better known Tapioca is made from processed manioc.

The natives invariably ate from a large plate of manioc mush *(shima)* made by stirring the flour and hot water into a stiff paste. They would dip a finger-full of *shima* into a smaller pot of relish which might consist of a tasty mouse, bird or one of the ubiquitous and scrawny village chickens. Thus appetisingly laced, the morsel would be conveyed by finger to mouth in a skilful movement.
We loved the *shima* which substituted for bread to a degree. It was excellent with soup or a tin of baked beans or for a real splurge, a tin of Norwegian sardines.

There being no shops or markets, canned foods had to be ordered six-monthly from S. Kopelowitz & Co of Livingstone. This involved sending a barge with the traditional sixteen paddlers and *kapitano,* downstream for 4 weeks and then hauling a full barge upstream for six weeks. Naturally all the missionaries on the station would make use of the same barge trip for replenishments.

Next to our house was a similar mud, wattle and thatched structure in which we stored manioc flour, peanuts and other less perishable foods. There being no lights in this building, on the occasions when Mother opened up the store, Walter and I used to enjoy wandering around in the dark and eerie atmosphere of bags and crude shelves, disturbing rats and perhaps coming across a stray cat on the prowl or guarding its newly born kittens.

One room contained an old box with carpenters' tools which had been used by my father. There were some large planes made of wood except for the metal blade fitted in position by a wooden chock, a wooden mallet and a few impressive saws and chisels. These would fetch a handsome price today as antiques. They were doubtless the tools given to him in Johannesburg as mentioned in one of his early reports.

My sister Margaret recalls times when Mother told us: "we have enough food to last a while but no money. Let us ask the Lord to supply our need".

On two such occasions there was a cheque in the post soon after.

An example of keeping one's sense of humour while facing pretty solemn circumstances, was Mother's remark once that we 'had onions and rice yesterday and for a change today we are going to have rice and onions'.

Mail would take four weeks by sea to Durban from the Australian Missionary Tidings in Melbourne, Australia, a further two or three weeks before reaching Livingstone by train and then six weeks up river to Balovale where the Chavuma "mail-boy" would collect our bag arriving 3 days later. A total of 4 months.

Though far from banks, money was useful in paying S. Kopelowitz & Co of Livingstone, tithing and as the cash component of the wages of workers and servants.

With the uses of cash being limited, part of wages were paid in kind. The most favoured items were coarse salt for adding to relish and fabric for sewing into clothes. Both of these were available from isolated trading stores but at a cost higher than the equivalent goods shipped direct from Livingstone.

I recall seeing a catalogue from Haddon and Sly, a wholesale company in Bulawayo, from whom certain equipment, such as a hair clipper set, was ordered from time to time.

The Balovale district had no shops in the usual sense. There was a trading store at Balovale owned by Bertram P. Rudge who with his wife Daisy, doubled as financially independent missionaries. The Rudges were, generous in their kindness towards less affluent co-missionaries, often sending them parcels of canned groceries, tomato sauce and the like.

At Chavuma there was a single trading store on the opposite bank of the river just below the falls, and one or two native-owned stores, one at an outstation run by a respected church elder.

The one near the falls was owned by a white man called Brice who took a native woman as wife. We would sometimes invite him to tea when we were picnicking at the mission summer house.

I recall that Walter and I were greatly intrigued by Brice's dentures which, natural or otherwise, were largely non-existent, so that his cheeks tended to get sucked inwards, to fill the gaps perhaps. The poor man would have had a long journey to find a dentist. Besides chewing *shima* and some meat there were not too many other reasons to be concerned.

Certainly the social life did not demand any cosmetic dentistry. In the event of a really bad toothache Bryce could have braved the forceps of the ever-handy Wallace Logan.

Fortunately Mother used her sewing skills to make us clothes. Often, the only material available was the blue print-cloth stocked by the traders for sale to the local natives.

Of course raising a family was more than feeding and clothing. As a single parent, Mother had, lovingly but firmly to enforce a discipline in the home.

I know that in my case, the absence of a father figure resulted variously either in disrespect for, or fear of any father figure.

Some disrespect, I suppose, arose from the absence of a dominant male, giving one an excessive amount of free rein. The fear of leaders came later when some of my customary free rein was not appreciated by teachers or headmaster and was swiftly penalised.

A devout Christian, Mother never flagged in her prayers, bible reading and worship. As she succeeded in teaching each of her children to read, we took turns to be the readers at the evening Bible session and prayers before retiring under our mosquito nets.

Quite apart from theology, Christian tenets, even in human terms, turned out to provide a sound framework for teaching and inculcating healthy discipline.

Growing up in an environment where one could get the impression that all white adults were born-again Christians and only natives and children had to be 'saved', it became slowly evident that missionaries were not always kind and sweet to each other, and that, albeit infrequently, were capable of displaying such human frailties as envy, pettiness and even loss of temper.

Of course Mother left us in no doubt that all required salvation including M.K.'s. She might justifiably have said - especially M.K.'s.

Family Bible reading and prayer were regular. The application of Bible stories was always practical rather than of the fairy tale kind and Mother was never dogmatic.

Most of our first reading lessons were unsurprisingly at Bible reading sessions. Being 16 months ahead of Walter it was natural that, having just struggled with a Bible passage, he once complained to Mother: "Why does it sound better when Gavin reads"?

That's one of the advantages of being the firstborn; there is no one to upstage you. At the same time, a determined younger brother constitutes a relentless competitor always panting just a few steps behind you, sometimes overtaking through sheer effort or special talent.

Travel was one of Mother's challenges which she handled with confidence, turning it into a missionary service.

Because there were no roads for motor transport until about 1940, travel away from the mission station meant walking or cycling along a footpath worn by bare feet braving the undergrowth. These were quickly overgrown in the tropics, so that it was not always easy to see which way the path went. Cycling meant dismounting often to traverse a fallen tree left by a passing elephant herd, or to cross a fast flowing river where a fallen tree trunk was the only bridge.

Seasonal flooding brought its difficulties too. An extract from co-missionary Wallace Logan's letter of 7th March 1934 gives a glimpse of the dangers.

"*Many of the plains were flooded and one had to walk through water from ankle deep to shoulder deep. At two rivers the log bridge broke while I was crossing. One bridge broke in front of me and a load-man went down through the broken part. His load caught on the broken bridge and there he hung with just his head above the water. The current was terrific and the bridge started to float away in pieces. For a few minutes things looked bad. The swift current and fear of crocodiles made one feel that human hope of being saved could not be expected. The rain was pouring down in torrents. I threw off my raincoat and sought to help the man caught with his head above the water. He shouted to me 'stay where you are, I will get out!' Now I could feel the logs under my feet going. By this time the native that had fallen through had climbed up and caught some of the logs and held them together while I made a few desperate jumps (to safety)*".

The hammock - the traditional form of transport

Logan goes on to describe a similar experience with a second log bridge and then adds:

"I mention these experiences that you may know that the dangers in this country are not only from the wild animals but scores of others..."

When tired from cycling in tropical heat, the missionary would use a hammock. Canvas hammocks were slung from the ends of a palm pole and had a covering of light wood trimmed with cloth and protective red fabric flaps which could be let down on each side to help in the constant fight against heat and sunstroke.

Hammock bearers, one at each end of the pole which rested on his shoulder on a soft pad, were deemed the most skilled of all the porters on any safari. Each bearer had one hand on the pole to keep it on his shoulder and in the other, held a *mufuka*, a fly whisk made from the tail of an antelope.

While carrying a passenger, the hammock men would wave their *mufukas* in a circular movement which, apart from fending off the eager and plentiful flies, seemed to provide a rhythm which maintained spirit and effort. Often they would chant a song ceremonially especially when arriving at a village camp or mission station. The leader would chant a phrase and his partner behind would respond. A song might go like this:

"I am Tomase and I know the path well. And I am Kambondo, I follow behind. We carry Kapalu first son of the missionary. With his brother and sisters they travel to Chingi.

The missionary will gather the folk in the villages. She will sing and will preach. She will make pleasant sounds. We will sing as she plays the white man's chisaji.

Village Headman (Nduna)

She will tell them they need to believe and be saved; that Kalunga has mercy for those who repent.

The villagers will be glad. The nduna has a present. A tender fat chicken to cook for the pot. The missionary too has a present; a bright coloured lihina, for the nduna's favourite wife.

His other wives will be envious to see her headdress.
The road is so rough. It becomes very hot. Kapalu gets heavy. But we are so diligent".

When the hammock carrying the missionary herself, emerged from the bush into the village clearing, the bearers would sometimes intensify their chanting. Flourishing the *mufuka* vigorously they would carry the hammock around the village several times chanting away and waving the *mufuka* in a kind of ecstatic announcement of NyaKapalu's arrival and as likely as not include a line in the chant advising the pot boy to get the kettle boiling for tea.

Mother loved her cup of tea. The native help knew this and it became customary to light a twig fire and boil the kettle even before the missionary arrived. Just as Mother was named after her eldest using the prefix *"Nya"*, so missionaries were also given nicknames by the natives. Mother was often known as *"Nya*-tea".

A clearing in a village was chosen as a campsite because wild animals were slightly less likely to constitute a threat than they would in the forest. The main reason however was that camping could in that way provide an opportunity for the preaching of the gospel to the heathen.

Whether or not the hammock bearers had announced our arrival in dramatic fashion, the advent of a white lady with four children and an entourage of porters was rare enough to ensure that every able-bodied villager and not a few crippled ones, quickly gathered around to stare at the wonderful luggage which soon transformed itself into a tent, folding camp, chairs and table, canvas wash basin, pedal organ and other curious evidence of *chindele's* wealth and resourcefulness.

The most inquisitive would be the naked children often with only a string of beads around their bellies and the younger women mostly bare-breasted. Crowding in on the 'white devils', they would squat motionless watching us thirstily drinking our tea.

The exchange of gifts referred to in the hammock bearers lyrics, would be a gentle reminder of what seemed to have become a custom especially when whites were around. If the visiting missionary was a little slow in producing the present for the *nduna*, a villager bearing a fowl with its legs tied, would make an ostentatious appearance signifying the moment for the trading of gifts had come.

Both during the colonial era and for many decades thereafter, Africa has been and remains a continent most adept at seeking handouts. Whether the tendency is an entrenched part of the culture or whether colonial practices actually encouraged dependence, thus inhibiting work ethic, is debatable.

Mother, whose sense of humour allowed her literary games with biblical text at times, once said, after noting the large numbers of begging hands reaching out to the passing train on her journey to Livingstone from Johannesburg, "Maybe that's what the Bible refers to where it states: *'Ethiopia shall stretch forth her hands'"*.

As for village chickens, while they were scrawny, they were very tasty and cost only sixpence. Their authentic flavour was not only due to the absence of artificial feeds such as fishmeal fed to many battery raised fowls in more industrialised countries, but notably due to the fact that no insect, earthworm or scrap of *shima*, was out of bounds to these birds.

The only restrictions they knew were the pecking order and the village pot simmering on the coals. Modern advertisers of chicken would have to admit that the African village brand of chicken is the most deserving of the label "free-range" of any fowl that ever squawked.

A strange looking vehicle with one wheel suitable for the footpath, a chair and two handles, fore and aft, known as the "callykoki", was used only occasionally. Its sturdiness made it too heavy and risky to manage across rivers balanced on a fallen tree trunk.

Most of the terrain travelled was very wild country. Seeing game grazing in the plains, snakes slithering away into the grass and a lion or elephant, were a normal part of the journey. Mother carried no gun.

One day she had cycled on ahead and when our hammocks caught up with her she stood resting quietly against her cycle motionless. A magnificent male lion stood on the side of a large anthill staring at us, now also as still as we could be. Eventually the lion sauntered off into the thick bush and we continued.

M.K.'s became blasé about the wild environment and when later visiting game parks in South Africa, tended to find the restriction against walking in the bush a bit tedious.

Wild honey was popular among the natives who used it in preparing beer. On one journey we came across some of the porters gathered round a tree which was buzzing with bees. Honey was oozing from a hollow in the trunk and the natives were reaching their hands deep into the hollow with impunity. Mother put her arm in withdrawing it hastily with twelve bee stings.

She attributed this reaction to the bees' suspicion of a white skin. In this politically correct day and age must we assume that bees were permitted to have racist preferences in those days?

For a long journey lasting a week or more we would have approximately ten porters. Loads including the tent, fly, folding organ, food and other camping equipment would be spread evenly so that no one carried a weight of more than 60 pounds. Food packs were the most popular because they got lighter each day. Mother was astute enough to re-allocate loads at intervals in the journey.

Crossing larger rivers would involve a canoe, actually a rugged dug-out carved from a single tree trunk. The shape was not always ideal and the tendency to roll sideways was common.

The volume of luggage and provisions not to mention many passengers including the bearers, usually meant several trips across crocodile infested waters with hippos and elephants not infrequent onlookers.

Though Walter and I grew up to love playing with canoes, from the age of about six, I had a fear of boating on a large stretch of open water. Having been old enough to be aware of my father's death from one of these boats, this was perhaps not surprising. Another experience may also have contributed to this fear.

The family was crossing the Zambezi to visit an out-school known as Mandalo. Sitting in the canoe, still beached, were the four of us each wearing a hat with an elasticated red sash protecting the back of our necks against sunstroke, Mother up front holding a pretty sunshade above her pith helmet, when the paddler, grasping his paddle shoved off from the beach, leaping into the stern.

Scarcely had we moved from the shore when the canoe turned over snapping the shaft of Mother's sun shade as it hit the water and depositing most of us in the river.

Fortunately it was close to the beach and shallow, so we dried out and ventured a second successful crossing.

In a letter on 28th November 1933, Mother describes a journey to a mission station in a remote part of Angola, much of which I can remember quite clearly.

We travelled by barge from Chavuma to Balovale and from there the normal way, by hammock across the plains to a Brethren mission station at Lungevungu (now spelled Lunguebungo).

Mother records our calling on the traditional headquarters and home of chief Kufuna, a cousin of the paramount chief Yeta. Kufuna had just acquired his own power boat, and proudly gave us a ride on the Zambezi. At the age of four, the small boat seemed so unsafe in comparison to the barge. Its speed and the fact that one sat so close to water level terrified me. It was only six months since my father's drowning in that river.

On several occasions when stopping for lunch on the river bank, we found crocodile eggs buried in the sand. These were later hatched at Chavuma in a zinc bath and it was sobering to observe the small crocs keeping their snouts just below the water at the edge of the bath and snapping at any fingers that might get within reach.

From Balovale, Walter and I travelled in our separate hammocks, the twins in another hammock and Mother on her bicycle, resorting to the hammock in the heat of the day.

It was on that leg of the journey that a hammock bearer assigned to carry a child's hammock was found to have the contagious disease leprosy. After some basic treatment he was sent home.

At one village en route, Mother heard that a man was divining. She went to watch. He seemed to be just playing with a feather from one of the ubiquitous fowls in the village, pushing it backwards on the ground. *"I asked him to let me do it but he refused, quickly finished and ran in to his house to hide the things (as usual) lest I should find out and reveal his deceit"*, she later wrote.

In our hammocks, hot and tired after a day's travel Walter and I became aware that the bearers were uncertain of the road, a euphemism for the footpath made solely (forgive the pun) by the passage of bare feet. My mother and the rest of the porters had moved faster and we seemed unable to catch up.

Now the sun was setting. Anxiety rose as darkness closed in. The strangely sobering sound of the African Nightjar *(Caprimulgus)* and the frightening call of a couple of hyenas were more chilling than the night air. The bearers laughed, but knowing their habit of nervous laughter when in danger, we derived no comfort from it. Soon it was the turn of the hyenas to begin laughing. The bearers fell silent at the menacing, eerie sound, starting with a low growl and rising to a higher pitched giggle. Not even the dance of fireflies was enough to distract us from the awareness of our unhappy predicament.

In her letter Mother records her thankfulness that the twins were with her and anxiety that my brother and I were lost in wildest Africa.

Hours later by the light of the moon and accompanied by the unique nocturnal sounds of tropical Africa, we felt considerable relief at virtually stumbling upon Lungevungu mission station, welcomed with joy by our prayerful mother.

On another trip to Lungevungu we journeyed with Wallace and Ruth Logan by barge downstream to Balovale, and at the confluence of the tributary Lungevungu, upstream to the mission station.

Spotting a large crocodile on a sandbank of the Zambezi the paddlers shouted *"Mwata, Mwata"*. Wallace Logan aimed and fired his rifle. The reptile jumped and then remained motionless on the sand. This was most unusual as crocodiles invariably flopped back into the water after being shot.

The paddlers cheered with glee at the demise of another of the creatures that killed or wounded so many of their people. The barge drew close to the sand bank and the paddlers disembarked and began tying bark rope around the creature so as to tow it behind the barge to the camping spot.

Suddenly, it blinked an eye and lashed its tail. The paddlers re-embarked in a split second and Wallace administered a final shot, after pushing the barge out a few metres from the shore.

At the camp site we all took turns to sit on the now, hopefully, deceased crocodile and took photographs.

With the skill of a surgeon the paddlers skinned and dissected the reptile. Whenever such opportunity offered, the natives inspected the contents of the stomach of a crocodile. On this occasion several handfuls of stones were found. Crocodiles are known to swallow stones which assist with digestion. However, on one occasion, the remains of a human hand and the shaft of a spear were found in the intestines of a crocodile killed near Chavuma.

At one camp, little Walter fell out of the barge and into the Lungevungu river disappearing beneath the surface in the crocodile infested waters. He was rapidly fished out dripping but already planning a strategy of one-upmanship based on his now superior experience.

Years later when the motor road reached Chavuma through the efforts of Wallace Logan, some limited travel could be done by truck as described in the chapter on Sakeji School.

Since so many people were involved in receiving medical attention, learning to read, hearing the gospel or travelling, Mother's work necessarily involved considerable management besides these functions.

Management writer Louis Allen's definition of management as planning, organising, leading and controlling accurately describes what my mother was frequently busy doing.

This widow's work included much supervision of the staff whom, as recorded, Mother had herself trained and who could not be left entirely to their own devices.

There was the ever present need for managing the unexpected, whether attending to a casualty with life threatening wounds, arguments between native factions or simply the illness of one of her children.

We had our share of whooping-cough, malaria, influenza and measles.

All these had to be managed often without equipment or the best medicines and without a doctor.

As in any team, Mother had to constantly liaise with the other missionaries on the station and take part in meetings concerning mission objectives, strategy and problem solving.

Her letters obtained from the archives of the Melbourne Bible Institute and the Australian Missionary Tidings, reveal that her work consisted of more than the mere execution of a set of duties allocated to her by her fellow missionaries. Nor was it a matter of only reacting to circumstances.

Clearly she engaged in strategic planning, goal setting and performance appraisal, though she had never received any training in these managerial concepts.

This appreciation of management principles enabled her to strike a balance of focus, and to avoid missing out areas or concerns that justified her attention. It enabled her to review and assess achievements .

Thus, her letters to, what one might call, her support constituency, often contained lists of objectives for which she had earlier requested prayer, systematically showing actual achievements against each one.

Her report of 31st January 1936 details a number of such goals and results. The simple yet effective format is illustrated, quoting one item:

Prayer Request:
For the setting up of the Lord's table at outstation.

Answers Received:

Two have been set up: Chingi and Kalasa opened.

The same letter reports:

"For a long time we have been very much concerned about distant villages as they do not hear the Gospel as often as we would like, some places perhaps only once in four or five years and some have never been reached. We have therefore mapped out routes throughout the whole territory, including every village and have called for volunteers from among the native Christians who will give a week of their time each year to preach the gospel. We have also promised to supply their food for the journeys. We are sending them out two by two working the territory systematically so that every village will be reached at least five times a year".

Mother's office was a place that fascinated us. A room of about 25 square metres, it had a window through which wages were paid to the staff and a large work-table dominated by an impressive structure of pigeon holes. There was a compartment for salt and shelves for rolls of fabric. A brass measuring yard was inlaid on the table surface.

As indicated elsewhere, employees were paid in cash for morning work and in kind, salt or cloth, for afternoon hours. This strengthened the incentive element in remuneration since money had limited use in the jungle.

The life of faith made the control of cash-flow challenging. Missionaries in the field had to practise a host of administrative skills besides their mainstream occupation.

This lady with a dressmaker's training and a theological diploma, had been blessed with a good brain and commonsense. She used to confide in me as her eldest son with no husband around and once told me of her technique - that there were moments when it was better to keep your mouth shut and risk being thought ignorant than to open it and remove all doubt.

When other missionaries or government officials used words with which she was not familiar, she would listen, apply some sound association of ideas and a measure of astute guessing, while others rushed in to display there superior knowledge. Finally Mother would review her guess in the light of what she perceived to be really critical in the situation and then express a view. Not only did her guesses usually prove correct, but focussing on what really mattered in the context, often made her seem like the wisest of them all; having modestly withheld judgement while they digressed.

With so much talent and personality Mother was no automaton. She had the ability to relax with her family and with friends.

She had a sense of humour which, next to her unshakable faith and confidence in the correctness of her career choice, helped to keep her balanced when many others might have been overcome with fear and, in human terms, by the abnormality of her situation.

She proved that one can be dedicated without being bigoted. Seeing the funny side of events and of behaviour, enabled her to relieve the pressure that a perpetual solemnity might otherwise have rendered intolerable.

As a family or with our Logan contemporaries Mother would often have us play charades in which a degree of acting or role-playing would provide cryptic clues to the word or phrase. Punning, witticism and other humour of a literary kind were regular features of family conversation.

She happily recounted stories of lighter moments even when speaking at report-back meetings to, what we might call, her constituency. It was probably this relaxed frankness that earned her the ill-informed description of 'frivolous', from one bigoted supporter. This remark had a sequel some years later.

Occasionally Mother would decide we needed a day of relaxation. This might mean a trip on cycles to a restful spot above the Chavuma falls where the mission had built a rustic summer house. We would take a picnic basket and of course, requirements for the mandatory tea. Sometimes we would share the day with the Logans.

A small lake near the main stream surrounded by golden sand made a great place for Walter and I to paddle a badly leaking canoe, trying to see if we could reach the opposite beach before sinking.

Among a group of rocks at the edge of the main river, was a lovely pool of clear, calm water with a soft sandy bottom. The natives, whose knowledge of natural conditions was usually respected, maintained that owing to the turbulent rapids above and below the pool, it would be safe from crocodiles.

We enjoyed swimming in the sparkling and delightful waters for a year or two until one day after a cool swim, and sitting safely back in the summer house enjoying our picnic lunch, we spotted a fierce looking crocodile specimen basking in the sun on the rocks, having just emerged from our pool.

Another wonderful spot to visit when Mother's workload permitted, meant crossing the Zambezi to the west bank and winding our way up a tributary to a fascinating place named Chanda where volcanic rock interrupted the surface flow of the tributary. The Chanda tributary, named Lufwiji, drained the flooded plains above and always teamed with fish.

Before descending steeply down to the Zambezi, the Lufwiji river actually dived under the volcanic barricade, coming up beyond the rock barrier about 600 metres above the confluence with the Zambezi.

The natural barrier presented a cul-de-sac into which the natives in two canoes and with a woven net strung between them, could noisily and with much splashing, herd shoals of fish, thus netting very satisfactory quantities with little exertion.

In the section of the river which ran underground, the volcanic rock had, over the ages been warn into grotesque shapes by the seasonal flood waters during which the river ran both underneath and over the rock barrier. The powerful currents and whirlpools had also smoothly drilled interesting holes in the lava some of which actually bored through the barrier down into the under-ground river below. Whirlpool holes ranged in diameter from a few centimetres to three or four metres and some were shallow. Many contained smooth and rounded stones which, having been swirled around, had no doubt played a role in the drilling process.

The natives often threw poisonous substances into the larger holes and collected the dead fish as they surfaced.

Walter and I discovered that by simply letting down a line with baited hook into a hole which connected with the underground river below, we could catch more fish than we knew what to do with. There were moments when the diameter of the fish exceeded that of the rock orifice. Thus the proverbial story of the 'one that got away' acquired a unique twist as the 'one that got stuck on the way'.

We caught species of fish from underground that we had never seen in Zambezi waters. I recall a scale-less, barbel type specimen with leopard-like spots on the soft skin and occasionally a similar species with tiger-like stripes. Both of these whiskered fish would make a buzzing sound vibrating the line as they were hoisted. Soup was all we could really use these trophies for.

The river reappeared, welling up in a deep basin of basalt about twenty metres wide and which had probably been the crater of the original volcano. It flowed over the lower lip of the crater and tumbled down to the Zambezi.

The unusual rock formation and features as well as the disappearance of an entire river underground, lent an air of mystique to Chanda. This feeling was accentuated by strange markings on the rocks which natives pointed out as being the, now petrified, spoor of various animals. Even stranger was the fact that there in central Africa, we were shown camel spoor, as well as that of other animals never seen by those who spoke to us.

A mark on the rock in the shape of a human footprint was, according to native legend, said to be that of the "Son of God". Whether this was a crafty interpretation designed to please the missionary or a genuine legend, we never knew.

Music and song, a part of any missionary's life, was, in Mother's case, also a loved form of recreation.

The small folding and portable Estey with two bellows pumped by foot action from which Mother magically urged the most harmonious and celestial of sounds, was replaced in 1938 by a later model with an extra octave and four stops namely, base and treble couplers and two stops for tonal effects, Vox Humana and Celeste.

The arrival of this proud model from H. Polliack and Sons in Johannesburg, added to our impression as children, that many good things were available in that city of gold down south. Warnings from adults that cities were also very wicked places, really only added to one's inquisitiveness.

Many happy moments enjoying music and learning to sing in harmony were spent around the organ. I recall listening to a native male voice choir being trained by Mother and being thrilled by the harmony. One member of the quartets had never broken his voice and his colleagues wanted him to sing the soprano which was certainly within his range. However NyaKapalu felt that would not give the unique sound of male voices in harmony and so our falsetto prodigy had to take the tenor part.

All of us were born with a musical appreciation and soon learned to pick out tunes on the keyboard. Knowing from singing that there were principally four parts to harmony I soon started playing the air with a couple of chords as accompaniment. Mother helped by showing me a few chords and sequences, she called cadences.

Learning anything you enjoy is always a fast journey, so before long I was playing recognisable hymns. Mother gave me a book by Sandy McPherson titled "Practical Harmony" which analysed harmony in a logical way. Before I knew much about written music I was remembering appropriate chords and sequences by their academic names: Tonic, Supertonic, Dominant Seventh, Sub- Dominant, Augmented and Diminished chords.

The range of voices which nature had allotted to the four of us happened to identify us naturally and without fuss, as Margaret - Soprano and Dorothy - Alto and later when our voices had matured, Walter - Tenor and me as Base; a ready-made quartet.

The missionary singer Jim Caldwell (Sakwimba) of Chitokoloki who had a stirring base-baritone voice, was the secret idol of all who loved singing. He and Nora his wife were always asked for their inspiring music wherever they went. Years later they ran a programme of gospel music on Lusaka radio.

Mother had a hand-wound gramophone and some gospel records of the nineteen twenties including what used to be called Negro spirituals, (a politically incorrect term today).

So the pop music we enjoyed included such highlights as: "Were you dere wen dey crucifaad ma Lo-erd?" and "It ain't ma brudder nor ma sista, butta me oh Lo-erd - standin' in da need of preaah".

We would sit for hours in rapture next to the old machine looking down the aperture from which the glorious sound seemed to emerge, after being magically picked up by the needle and wafted along the flexible hollow arm into the innards of this scientific marvel.

The regional native chief, named Kufuna, a cousin of the great paramount chief Yeta, once visited our home and gave us a record by the famous boy Soprano, Ernest Lough, of "Oh for the Wings of a Dove" and "Hear My Prayer Lord". I also remember having a small disc with two xylophone pieces one being a minuet, the other a foxtrot.

Kufuna was a professing Christian. Mother wrote of the impression this highly placed chief had on his people. Two black evangelists sent out from Chavuma called on him and were amazed by the humility shown by Kufuna *"who called us into his home and gave us food, we who are unworthy even to talk to him"*.

So we grew up with a pretty good mix of gospel, Southern spirituals and classical music. But Christian choruses were our main diet. We learned many from Mrs. Ruth Logan who taught them with appropriate hand actions.

The most well-known of these would have been: "We are building day by day in our work and in our play...." in the singing of which one would, for example, place one fist upon another to signify the layers of bricks. The one about shunning evil: "Get them out get them gone, all the little rabbits in the field of corn" was accompanied by a vigorously gestured shooing out of the naughty rabbits.

The missionaries Gladys, Doris and Daisy occasionally arranged a party at their house. It was there we learned to play, London Bridge, Ring-a-Ring of Roses, Musical Chairs and similar children's games popular at the time. Receiving a kiss from Doris Mitchell in Postman's Knock was the first one I remember from anyone but my mother. 'Auntie' Doris seemed to enjoy it too.

7. *Faith versus Superstition*

It is not difficult to see the missionary effort in Central Africa as the frontline of the conflict between faith and superstition. While superstition is alive and well in so called Christian countries, these opposing forces are rarely seen so starkly at war as in the backdrop to this story.

It must be admitted that some religions seem to contain enough mumbo jumbo and cultural ritual as to be, themselves, not very different from superstition. There is of course an element of the supernatural common to both faith and superstition.

Ironically, missionaries who came with a message about the Almighty wishing to redeem human beings, and who's Son had performed many wonders and miracles on earth, were often seen by the local heathen people as a little slow to perceive the hand of the supernatural in events. The missionaries seemed to show little respect for the powers of the ancestral spirits.

Actually, while convinced of the folly of these superstitions, the missionaries were properly concerned about their powerful effect on the populace and consequent hindrance to the propagation of the Christian Gospel.

On mission stations, the refugee victims of superstitious practices were a constant reminder of the prevalence of the occult in the population at large. On the metaphorical river of my mother's missionary experience, however, there were strong undercurrents threatening to break out on to the surface as eddies and whirlpools.

Missionaries working at this spiritual battle-front were vitally conscious of the ongoing warfare as clearly indicated in their daily language and writings. Perhaps more so than many in the Church at large, these were truly the Christian soldiers referred to in the well-known hymn.

Superstition in combination with the power of the witchdoctor was a daunting force which held many natives in a grip of awe and fear.

In a circular issued just five months before his death, my father writes about an itinerary to the Manyinga river district:

"I journeyed through the jungle forest plains for 24 days carrying a message of salvation to the natives in the most backward part of the Balovale district. The Gospel was preached to the VaLwena, VaLunda, VaChokwe, VaLoze and VaLuwi people.

Much that was really primitive was noticed here. Native idols and divining contrivances were much in evidence both on the person and in and around the huts and enclosures. The natives in many cases were clothed in skins and the children fled from the villages at the sight of a white face".

His letter goes on to describe how elephants intent on devouring the little millet planted by the natives, *"were in abundance everywhere".* The villagers asked him to stay and shoot the elephants.

He writes of a native who on accepting the Christian message tore from his throat the lion-claw necklace he had been wearing to keep him in health.

On the same trip to Manyinga, my father was shown a piece of skin used for divining. The hide came from a buffalo which, after being shot and thought dead, had, it was said recovered, got up

Fred Barnett & helper:
House and relics of a deceased villager.

and killed his hunter. Skin from such a strong animal was powerful magic-making material.

In a circular dated 7th March 1934, Wallace Logan tells of experiences on a 500 miles preaching excursion to villages where he was troubled by the incidence of spirit worship with its *"filthy practices"*.

He writes:

"In one village the woman in the hut next to my tent became demon-possessed about midnight. I have never heard anything like it in my life. It was like being next to Satan himself. Her shouts and screams just sent chills down my back."

A converted native, with Logan, began shouting out the gospel combining strangely with the woman's screams. In a moment the woman was calm and the eerie noise subsided.

Effigy representing an ancestor

In a letter dated 10th December 1935, Mother wrote to Dr Nash quoting a Christian native elder in a sermon:

"In the past we loved just the desires of our own hearts. Our eyes were closed. We were in darkness. We danced and beat drums. We divined and worshipped idols. When God saw that we were near death and hell, then the Saviour was sent".

The dancing and drum beating referred to, was common among villages especially those some distance from the mission station. Dancing was associated with certain traditional rituals and also with seasonal abundance of beer-making ingredients such as honey. The rhythmical sound of drums and singing wafted on the wind from villages across the Zambezi was eerie and somehow depressing to a young boy of six retiring under his mosquito net for the night.

The preferred chords and chord sequences in African music made for a distinct idiom of its own.

We were brought up to react to the sounds as heathen since they were associated with the dancing rituals and various forms of wickedness.

The very strong impression this music made on my childhood memory was illustrated by the eerie feeling experienced when listening, in 1982, to a record of genuine African music types compiled and produced by the talented Professor Hugh Tracy of Rhodes University, in Grahamstown. Hearing the sample of Lwena music featured on the disc, gave the illusion of a powerful time warp, and I felt strangely transported back to Chavuma.

Drums were carved out of a single piece of timber. The tom-tom type was conical with charred decorative art and cowhide stretched tightly across the top end. A similar shaped drum but a little longer and usually narrower was the *ngoma pwita.*

This interesting drum had a bamboo reed inserted into the hollow tube, with one end fixed to the underside of the skin diaphragm. The instrument was played by gripping the greased reed and sliding the hand up and down it, emitting a loud vibrating sound with the inward thrust and producing a slightly different tone from the outward pull. The sound was distinctive and in contrast to the beat of the more ordinary drums.

Another drum style had no hide diaphragm at all. Like the others it was carved out of a solid tree trunk and hollowed out, but its shape was rather like that of a purse, wider at the bottom than at the top.

The resonance resulted from the clever hollowing done entirely with a native made knife. This drum often had some rough metal strips threaded through loose metal tubes and fixed into the top narrow side to give a rattle sound when the flat sides of the drum were beaten. This drum was occasionally suspended from a pole and carried around the village by two men, the one at the rear beating as they walked.

Almost every hut in the typical village had idols outside the front door, comprising images and effigies representing the ancestors. Mother describes them in letter 16th July 1938:

"Their gods are truly 'the work of men's hands'. Some are formed of mud to resemble animals while some are simply sticks standing up out of the ground. Others again are carved from wood in various shapes".

Food was left for them in a form of sacrifice, despite the obvious fact that dogs, cats and fowls were the real beneficiaries. Giving up the idols was expected of any one who was converted to Christianity.

Reporting on a village itinerary Mother wrote on 12th June 1935,

"...there were those who showed determination to be done with the old life. We saw idols pulled out of the ground, a pipe smashed, charms taken off by those who had been wearing them and some secret idols brought out of the house by the owner".

Similarly in her letter of 31st January 1936, reporting on the success of a campaign to reach remote villages by sending out voluntary native preachers, she refers to volunteers bringing back *"idols and fetishes that the natives, who have turned to the Lord, have given up".*

Mother described a native woman who, on accepting the Gospel, removed a charm of wild animal teeth or claws from the neck of her baby worn to help the baby to learn to walk quickly.

A common custom among the natives was to mark their faces in a form of tattooing. Lines and diagrams were cut into the flesh leaving blackened scars that were supposed to make the wearer more attractive to the opposite sex. Missionaries opposed the practice as heathen and in time a clear face became one of the outward signs of Christian influence.

According to a rigid custom the graves of natives who had not accepted Christianity, were decorated with the material possessions of the departed. The affluence of the deceased could be assessed by the height of the jumble of rusty metal trunks and plates nailed to poles and whatever wisps of clothing still fluttered in the breeze above his resting place.

However, graves were not peaceful places to which a loved one might resort out of respect for those who had experienced the shadow of death. Death was shrouded in fearful mysteries and associated with evil spirits. Annoying the ancestors was something to be avoided.

So it was that during one journey coming across another familiar burial site, we were impressed by the magnitude of possessions that the deceased had left behind in this case. It was a veritable battery of artefacts ranging from an old bicycle to a cracked cup and from the horns that once belonged to a bull, to a lethal looking spear.

Mother, whom it will be remembered from a previous chapter, had shown little fear of the *mukishi,* stopped to photograph the display of chattels and walked confidently towards this stacked exhibition of materialism and superstition. Here was substantial testimony to the primitive heathen practices which the missionary had to penetrate, figuratively wielding the 'sword of the spirit'.

As if from nowhere, a crowd had gathered to watch the white woman defy the ancestors, the witchdoctors and the centuries of ancient tradition.

Mother reached out and lifted the lid of an impressively large trunk whose rusty hinges let out a painful yell startling the audience.
Undaunted by sound of the screaming hinges, Mother leaned forward to look inside the trunk. This was more than just curiosity. Her courage might demonstrate to the superstitious onlookers that they were being unnecessarily held in fear by the ruthless village elders and their

traditions.

As she lowered her head, a squadron of furious hornets flew off their nest inside the trunk and straight for her face. She jumped back brushing the hornets away and emitting a cry of surprise. The trunk lid fell back emitting another eerie yelp.

When Mother turned around there was not a native in sight. They had rushed off to the village breathlessly recounting the missionary's encounter with the evil spirits.

The missionary objective was not simply a matter of discrediting belief in the paranormal, but rather selecting which of those beliefs were "of the devil" and therefore spurious, and distinguishing them from a different sort of supernatural in God's economy. Not an easy challenge.

While the missionary's theology contained the incentive of a heaven to be gained and the penalty of a hell to be shunned, the local customary beliefs were enforced with penalties for the current life, some of them extremely gruesome.

Witch doctors had enormous power and played a role in the village existence pattern in which the unwanted aged were eliminated, especially when food was short as a consequence of drought, fire or locusts.

In a reference to Kalasa out-school in July 1932, my father wrote
"murders are common here".

A detached view might see these practices as just one part of the population balancing role which these natural disasters, savage animals and disease, played in the ecological scenario. Certainly there were latent population pressures arising from irresponsible procreation and the limited agricultural activities of the natives.

Any disaster had to be attributed to evil spirits who in turn required a human vessel through whom to bring about calamity. So when lightning struck, burning down a hut, a culprit had to be identified. The ritual calling of names enabled such identification. Witchdoctors invariably identified someone whose presence was either a burden or was no longer wanted in the village.

The practice created an opportunity for a villager wishing to be rid of anyone, to suborn the witchdoctor into using his magic to select a desired victim.

The commonest naming method used by witchdoctors at the time, employed an interesting piece of equipment consisting of a waxed piece of string threaded through two holes pierced in a small spherical gourd or seed pod about six centimetres in diameter. The string ends were held one in each hand and with a free finger the seed pod was pushed upwards along the threaded string as a name was called. If the pod fell back to the lower end of the string, the name called was innocent. However should it stick halfway down the string, the name called was that of the guilty party.

The culprit villager, usually an aging woman, was driven into the forest, where, until mission stations established refuge for such luckless folk, wild animals or starvation would play their role in natural population control. Ironically it was rogue carnivores no longer able themselves, to hunt with the pack, that skulked around villages looking for easy pickings.

Most mission stations were prepared for these refugees and gave them medicine, food and a clean hut to live in. This Christian kindness did not discourage the savage cruelty, against which missionaries preached vociferously.

In doing so they made themselves unpopular with the practitioners who did pretty well out of the system and so had a vested interest in maintaining their power.

In a joint letter dated 1st July 1932 my father tells how he and Logan came upon a diviner named Samalombwe seeking to identify the evil spirit which had caused the illness of a child.

"He threw a seed-box (lusangu) up and down a piece of string as he called the names. If the seed box remained suspended on the string, the named spirit was the offender".

Logan discovered the means of deception: *"By pulling the string tight, the seed box remained suspended."*

Shortly after he invited the surrounding villagers to attend an important gospel meeting at which the deceit of the powerful purveyors of witchcraft would be exposed.

The indomitable Wallace Logan had a talent for making his sermons interesting and had an appreciation of the dramatic. This talent was later emulated to good effect by his sons and daughters.

I recall the event clearly. The Chavuma assembly hall was packed and the atmosphere was electric. The pews were built of clay brick and plastered. One aisle down the centre divided men from women, a concession to native custom. The Lwena were a male- dominated society.

The pews nearest the raised pulpit had timber tops and formed a square. Missionaries all sat on one side of the square with the ladies wearing their regulation hats, not in this case as protection against the sun but in compliance with the Biblical injunction that women cover their heads in church. Native women wore colourful hair nets of satin or an old rag depending on their state of affluence.

The service was, as usual, conducted entirely in Lwena. The harmoniously sung hymns and prayers over, Logan mounted the pulpit, read an appropriate scripture condemning sorcery and witchcraft and proceeded to point out that those who deceive others do so because their propositions are false. The truth needs no tricks.

He then announced that the most common routine by which the false servants of evil pointed out culprits suiting their own ends, was a simple trick anyone could learn to do and he was about to prove it.

Suspending the string ends between his hands and holding up the instrument so that all could see the seed-pod, he invited volunteers to be named. There were no takers. He explained that he could make the seed-pod stop or fall at will and calling the name of Frances, his eldest daughter, he deliberately made the seed-pod fall. He then said he would make the seed-pod stick for someone else and called twin sister Esther's name. The seed-pod stayed up. The congregation was spell-bound, catching their breath in fear and wonderment.

Logan had to explain that his daughter Esther was not an evil spirit and that in fact anyone in the hall could be the victim of a deceitful diviner using this trick.

Out in the villages many a curse was rained down upon the missionary for this artful strategy in the 'good fight'.

The challenges of debunking superstition while seeking to introduce Christian practices, such as Communion, to the converted, may be better appreciated in the light of an account in my mother's letter dated 10th December 1935, where she quotes a Christian native whose daughter had recently been converted.

"When my daughter was baptised, her husband who is headman of the village went all around telling people of this unheard action on the part of his wife. He hated her very much for being baptised. Then when she went to break bread at the Lord's table, her husband said 'she is very bad, for she has gone to eat the flesh of a person and to drink the blood at the Lord's table' ".

Christianity's own debate over the fine distinction between *tran-substantiation* and *consubstantiation* would, alas, hardly be a helpful factor in this instance.

Interestingly, literal understanding of the words "this is my blood", may have been behind the behaviour of a believer in fellowship (Nyamalesu) who was often observed to stand up in church after receiving the cup, go over to the window and spit out the communion wine she had sipped. The matter was duly handled by the elders.

Wallace Logan used his penchant for dramatic illustration not only in the war on superstition but also in support of Christian teaching.

The apparent impossibility of God gathering together all the saved alive and resurrecting those whose bodies were scattered in the dust or lying at the bottom of the sea, on that future day when Christ would come again (the *parousia)*, was handled this way.

Logan ground up some iron filings which, having been shown to the congregation, he scattered between pews all over the hall. *"If I a mere human being can collect and recover all these filings, then you must believe that God could do the same with his redeemed"*, said Logan.

Incredulity showed on the faces. He produced a powerful magnet and proceeded to collect all the filings pew by pew and showed the audience the filings clinging to the magnet in the way that the *"saved will be caught up"*. He showed them a receptacle of filings that was now full once more. The message was not lost on the hearers.

On another occasion seeking to warn those who rejected the Gospel, Logan illustrated the characteristics of the fire and brimstone associated with hell, *"the fire that is not quenched"*.

He invited the congregation to join him outside the hall where he threw some damp calcium carbide on the ground and lit a match. The acetylene gas generated by the combination of water and calcium carbide burns fiercely, as every student of physical science knows. However he then invited anyone to put out the flames by pouring water on the burning carbide. Far from extinguishing the flame the resultant massive increase in acetylene gas caused a virtual explosion of flame to the horror of the congregation, not to mention one impressionable M.K.

In the hostile environment of heathen superstition, faith was not simply a matter of winning people over to a better code of living but, certainly initially, very much a matter of weaning them away from a distinct and palpable voodoo-like bondage.

There was, of course, evidence of changed outward behaviour on the part of those who accepted the gospel. Not only did they tend towards clothing that did a better job of covering, but they became tidier.

Mother wrote on 16th July 1938 after a trip in Manyinga which was seen as an area in the grip of heathendom.

"It was a happy occasion when we arrived at one of the out-schools and refreshing to see the tidy well kept and large village space where the gospel halls are built especially after spending so much time in the dirty villages".

The word *faith* had poignant meaning for these evangelical front-line troops. Faith was not just a creed. It was the key that unlocked their courage and unleashed commitment and tenacity. It was, in fact, the engine that dealt with such practical matters as where the next meal was coming from, rescue from danger and peace of mind.

There was a practical significance to what the Brethren called the life of faith, which meant no regular stipend or salary.

Mother's letter of 29th December 1938 read:

"You will be interested to know that the Christmas gift arrived here on Christmas day and of course caused much rejoicing. May the Lord bless all the dear ones who so faithfully give of their means and provided such generous help for those of us who are out here away from our relations, He will reward...."

There was scant chance that any hypocrisy on the part of missionaries would survive long in this environment. Sincerity and faith were tested daily.

As one of the naturally questioning Children of Chavuma growing up in this atmosphere of profound faith and calm assurance, I cannot state that miracles were a daily occurrence. Some remarkable outcomes that could feasibly be viewed as answers to prayer are recorded in this narrative. What I did see around me was people who were, outwardly, untroubled by doubt, and who succeeded most of the time in displaying happiness and often joy, even in the most adverse circumstances.

It must be understood that when I write of my impressions of matters concerning doctrine of the church I grew up in, I do so purely on the basis of memory and without any authority or mandate on the subject.

The African mission field presented a number of doctrinal problems requiring practical decisions which would not arise 'at home'.

The almost universal polygamy among native men was one of these. Converts were told that to walk the Christian path they had to have only one wife. This raised questions concerning what criteria to apply in abandoning all but one wife and also about hardship for the discarded wives. Some felt the rule applied only to those who were elders in the Church in recognition of the Apostle's instruction that elders be the "husband of one wife". Others were of the view that Paul's injunction simply meant an elder should be married.

Fred referred to this and other matters in his letter of 1st July 1932 and records some of the questions raised by the natives, for example:

Can we be saved if we have several wives?
Must we put some down to believe?
Must we put down child wives?
Can we be saved if we are engaged to a heathen girl?
We are accustomed to divining. Our ancestors believed in the power of spirits and we have seen wonderful things done by them. How can we put such beliefs down?
Must we settle these before believing?

Some considerable wisdom was required to handle issues like this. Owing to the practices which missionaries advocated or condemned it was quite easy to identify villages where the headman was converted. As reported by Mother after visiting Manyinga, villages were patently cleaner where an out-school or a Christian testimony had been established.

Most obviously, there were no idols (ancestral images) in a village having a Christian influence. There would be no common pipe. This pipe, similar to the oriental hookah, was a coffee-pot shaped gourd with a baked clay tobacco holder attached by a bamboo stem with another stem for inhaling. The smoke was filtered through water inside the gourd to cool it.

The pipe was often smoked communally in a hut having open sides which served as a village social lounge. The pungent smell of the strong tobacco became an indicator of a "heathen" village .

Although missionaries were more concerned about the state of the soul than appearance and dress, the more extreme forms of dress or undress and behaviour such as dancing and *mukishi* parade, were frowned upon.

Even the women's headdress of mud plaster, common in Africa, was less likely to be seen in a 'Christian' village.

At a report-back meeting in Melbourne someone remarked to Mother: "I suppose it must make it all worthwhile just to see the heathen black people washed and dressed properly after joining the church!"

Mother hastened to direct the questioner back to the main objective, explaining that it would be pointless to go out to tropical Africa with its malaria and other hazards unless people's hearts and lives were being genuinely changed.

This truth has been expressed many times since, as the world has despaired of Africa's efforts to govern itself despite having adopted the garments of Western culture and other cosmetic trappings of what we call civilisation.

Occasionally a man had to be asked to take his hat off in church. *"Fumisa litepa"* an elder would cry out, as an unsuspecting man would walk down the centre aisle hoping all could see his magnificent European style headgear purchased at great cost from the trading store, only to be required to doff the newly acquired prestige symbol.

While native women usually wore a brightly coloured satin *lihina,* the missionary ladies sported creations sent to them by kind supporters but which were not guaranteed to be at the forefront of fashion.

The form of the Brethren worship service (communion) was unique in that there was no obvious leader or detailed programme.

The only mandatory objectives were that the sacraments would be distributed exactly as they were on the night instituted and there would be worship. The rest of the proceedings would be spontaneous contributions from male participants by way of a hymn selection, a prayer of praise or an exposition of the Word. The Brethren believed the Holy Spirit actually guided such worship services.

There was clearly a sensible effort on everyone's part not only to select hymns and scriptures relevant to the essential object of a communion service namely to "show forth His death", but also to develop and pursue, what we might refer to as, an ancillary theme for that particular service. Thus each contribution would add new insight, understanding or devotion to a perceptible theme, despite the fact that no one ever announced what the theme was to be, and despite the intellectual limitations of many of the participants.
A recipe for chaos? Surprisingly, inappropriate contributions or disorder were an extremely rare occurrence. A detached observer was once on record as asking who was the genius that put together that splendidly rounded off programme and got each participant to prepare and deliver their relevant contribution to what must have been a well rehearsed programme?

What is perhaps more surprising is that barely literate native believers could participate in such an apparently purposeful, orderly and artistically appealing service, with acceptable facility.

Occasionally human ego would spoil the effect, and I recall an occasion when two rather distinct ancillary themes, Christ's resurrection and his second coming seemed to be vying with each other for position. A wise but frank brother rising, said: "I must confess to some confusion as to which of the two aspects we are considering in our worship this morning". He then humbly but firmly selected the resurrection for its closeness to the main purpose of the communion service. The meeting proceeded with obvious unanimity from that point.

Baptism was carried out by immersion, the only mode mentioned in scripture, where the process of immersion and emergence is said to symbolise death and resurrection.

The Brethren held the logical view that the more convenient mode of sprinkling water on an unwitting infant's head, as a supposed alternative, completely ignores the intended symbolism and is devoid of any declaration on the part of the infant

Immersion at Chavuma, meant that baptismal services had to be conducted on a bank of the Zambezi.

The congregation would "gather at the river" (if one may slightly misappropriate the wording of the well-known hymn).

Baptism Scenes

A more delightful venue one could hardly imagine. The calming sound of the mighty river flowing swiftly past, the crystal clear water and the inviting ripple of waves smoothing the white sand of the beach, made for an eminently more aesthetic baptismal facility than the concrete or tiled pools built beneath the floor boards of chapel platforms.

There was only one blemish. The ever present danger of crocodiles could potentially turn a baptism into a disaster. At Chavuma this risk was minimised by erecting a protective network of saplings or bamboo in a semi-circle on the river side, just deep enough off-shore.

So the typical baptismal scene at Chavuma was of a fully dressed missionary standing waist-deep in the Zambezi and immersing the candidate. As each of the baptised rose dripping from the water, the congregation broke into singing lustily the hymn chorus *Kava kava* ("follow, follow, I will follow Jesus...").

My brother and I were baptised in this fashion at the same spot.

The power of the superstition and of the diviners, sadly did not disappear totally on conversion or baptism and such instances of reversion under pressure were matters of concern and prayer.

The same sense of loss occurred when a faithful member decided to go south to the, then, Union of South Africa, usually to seek wealth by working on the famed gold mines *(mayini).*

This was equivalent to the prodigal son going into a far country for the same reason. I suppose the Christian influence as well as the comparatively affluent lifestyle of the missionaries, inevitably had to trigger off some desire for the fruits of a civilised way of life even though this attitude was discouraged as being a manifestation of materialism.

Unlike the returning prodigal, the erstwhile faithful, came home conspicuous with the trappings of wealth in the form, perhaps, of a bicycle, smart clothes and so forth, often showing signs of his absence from mission influence and of the profligacy available in *Jwanesbegi*.

Another cause for grief was the occasional defection to the *Chitavala* (a corruption of the word Watchtower).

In those times the Watchtower Society left its native adherents largely unsupervised so that they tended to mix African customs with the tenets of the sect. In the Chavuma area there were reports that Chitavala often baptised converts in sand. It was assumed that danger from crocodiles had influenced this practice.

The movement fell foul of the Northern Rhodesian government, as they later did of Kaunda's government, allegedly because they refused allegiance to a human authority.

There is a reference in my father's letter dated 1st July 1932 to a *"false teacher who stood up dramatically at Chavuma and propounded strange and fantastic doctrines. After gaining a few followers this diversion failed."*

It was unlikely that a missionary who harboured serious doubts and questions about his beliefs would leave home and relatives for the inhospitable environment of Africa.

So while any personal doubts among missionary folk were not in evidence to the M.K. generation, most Christians will admit that belief and faith are not the easy ride one might hope for.

Even though cocooned in the faith from the cradle, intellect inevitably raised questions. At first a child asks questions in innocence. As the child grows older the number of questions increases but so too does the awareness that doubting Thomases are not lightly welcomed and inhibitions against free questioning can easily develop. However earnestly one was taught biblical truth, this was unconsciously filtered through the faculties of rationality.

This process, in turn, produces what Festinger describes as *cognitive dissonance.*

Festinger's Theory of Cognitive Dissonance postulates that individuals, when presented with evidence contrary to their 'world- view' or situations in which they must behave contrary to their 'worldview', mentally experience something he called "cognitive dissonance".

This discord between what one is told to believe and what one sees happening is, ironically, stimulated by a more comprehensive knowledge of the translated bible, revealing inconsistencies which should not be there given divine literal inspiration. Some inconsistencies of course have arisen from the human factor in translations which often tended to be underplayed. Brethren speakers often used other English translations to clarify meaning obscured by translation, and the "original Greek" was often quoted, to provide the intended meanings. A common example was the three Greek words, each with a different shade of meaning, but all of which have been translated into English as "love".

It did of course seem more than just a pity that a record as important as God's word had been allowed to be subjected to imperfections through human weakness in translation.

Learning of the existence of the "apocryphal" books and the question of their exclusion from 'holy writ', was another disturbing aspect.

The manner in which, the very human members of The Third Council of Carthage in A.D.397 and the Council of Trent in A.D.1546, made momentous decisions as to which books to include in the Holy Bible, is not reassuring to the enquiring young mind, especially as these decisions are not equally supported by all Christian denominations.

Mother was always meticulously honest in trying to answer such querying. She never dogmatically waved them aside.

This impressed us. Her example of willingness to admit, in the midst of such steadfast faith, that she did not have all the answers, was a more attractive and endearing response than some of the more dogmatic or contrived answers one heard at times.

The influence of devout parents and the missionary school saw many children following the faith. Opportunities or encouragement for questioning the faith in that atmosphere were few indeed. You could reach the age of 10 or 13 and never meet an 'unsaved' white person or one following a different religion except the occasional government officials who unfortunately often seemed to be such jolly liberated fellows.

After Sakeji School, when M.K.'s moved to high schools elsewhere, exposure to the ungodly and some of their pleasures wrought a few casualties in Brethren terms.

At the same time the high standards of discipline and commitment paid off even for the doubters, as evidenced in the extraordinarily consistent career successes of so many of Sakeji's pupils.

It must be remembered that the Brethren interpretation was opposed to vain repetition and what one might call the more superstitious and ritualistic trappings of religion. They queried every practice and dogma that was not expressly found in scripture and encouraged critique and discussion at least to that extent.

One of the most draconian elements in the teaching and which had a powerful effect, especially on missionary children, was the fear of not being ready for the second coming of Christ. Often the fear persisted even after having made a profession of faith.

At the end of a gospel service in which the dire torments awaiting those who were not saved were forcefully and emotionally preached, there were some children who tearfully wondered whether they were in fact "ready" and were inclined to go through the believing process again. One particularly frightening aspect was the often repeated warning of finding your parents and perhaps a brother taken up to heaven at the second coming while you were left behind for eternal hell.

This was of course taught sincerely as biblically based evangelical truth and by prayerful parents who above all wanted their own children to enter the fold.

Its power over the young mind was demonstrated by the frightening experience of arriving home and finding everyone had gone out and the guilty fear that you might indeed be left behind.

M.K.'s were not totally brainwashed, nor, by and large, were they an irrational bunch of kids. It was acceptable to ask why God wanted things done in a certain way. Where a humanly rationalised answer was not available, as in the case of the question: "Why does an omnipotent God make us able to sin if he abhors it that much?", one was often told that we cannot understand everything God does and the Bible states: "Shall not the God of all the earth do right?"

Why for instance did God allow my father to be drowned, his dedicated missionary calling reduced to 3 years in printing and another three at Chavuma, his unrecovered body to be taken probably by a crocodile and leaving a widow and four young children in uncivilised and dangerous tropical Africa?

Well, it was enough to know that nothing was outside of God's planning though he was held to have a direct will and also permissive will. The permissive will sometimes appeared to allow actions and events which seemed at variance with Christianity's main themes and purposes.

Mother sometimes summed up this debate by quoting: "Who hath known the mind of the Lord or who hath been his counsellor?" (Romans 11:34). A gentle reminder that even though we are naturally possessed of the healthy faculties of logic and reasoning, if we believe in the creator-God of the Bible, there has to be a certain arrogance in presuming to know better than He.

Personally, the most reasonable exposition of the puzzling questions, was that the freewill given to humans (and presumably to the Devil) as well as the permitted randomness of events, does suggest that from time to time God voluntarily places a measure of self-imposed limitation on his own divine omnipotence.

Many would have difficulty with this view in that it is seen to minimise the Almighty even if the limitation is self-imposed. Yet the Bible does provide some indication that the universe is not yet totally subjugated and that there are anti-God forces which have some considerable rein and which perhaps perpetrate disasters which we attribute to God. It would be consistent with that understanding, that many of those disasters could hurt the very people God might be expected to protect.

We did experience happenings very close to miracles especially where a need for food or an event affecting travel or major decision was prayed for earnestly. Gifts would appear from the most unlikely sources who knew nothing of our plight. Even non-essential
things, but which my mother had prayed for were, amazingly delivered at times.

She writes on 3rd August 1940:

"We had a lovely answer to prayer this morning. We had prayed for eggs and meat as we had neither and about two hours later a man appeared with both".

There was no means by which the need could have been made known, no telephones and no fast transport.

With no shop within 1000 miles and little money anyway, the idea of a widow providing a tricycle for her children who envied those seen in picture books, seemed like pie in the sky.

The only course was to tell your children that if God wanted them to have a trike he would do something about it, and to pray that he would indeed honour their faith.

My brother and I had converted an old pram formerly used by all four of us, into a 'car' (something we had not seen except in magazines) and we thrashed the remaining life out of it careering down slopes and laughing hilariously as we crashed into a ditch.

Unexpectedly one day the postman, returning from his weekly 75 kilometre walk to Balovale, carried over his shoulder a lovely blue and red tricycle. The District Commissioner' daughter had outgrown her tricycle and his wife wondered if the Barnett kids would like to have it. Would they just!

Thus without in any way ruling out coincidence in the sequence of events, faith was given, let us say, a sporting chance.

The King James or Authorised version of the Bible was beloved by the Brethren. The graceful and majestic language of that era is indeed irresistible poetry. For people who devoured the scriptures as their daily bread and learned it in that idiom, it would understandably be difficult to realise that the version had no special divine status of its own.

For some, revering the A.V. became more than a fixation. The story is told of someone joining in a debate on the use of other translations, whose contribution was: "If the Authorised Version was good enough for the Apostle Paul then its good enough for me".

Most Brethren knew that italics used in the A.V. are 'glosses' inserted by translators to help with understanding the transliteration and therefore cannot be described as inspired in the narrow sense.

Imagine our M.K. grins when a sincere but naïve speaker at a worship service in Johannesburg, after reading his selected verses said, in his 'h'-dropping accent, "I want you to carefully notice the words in hitalics. When the 'Oly Spirit puts words in hitalics, 'e means us to pay special hattention to them". The brother then proceeded to base an entire message purely on the italicised insert.

Attendance at Sakeji, the school for M.K.'s, where scripture was a major subject, ironically reduced any tendency to blind belief. While the teachers were of course good Brethren stock and dedicated missionaries in their own right, they naturally tended to be more academic than the average parents of M.K.'s. The educational environment understandably and inevitably insinuated the acceptability of questioning and supported a modicum of rational search, even for scientific proof.

I suppose it was the tendency to question, that made extra-biblical testimony to events described in the Bible so interesting. For example I was fascinated by stories that the supposed remains of Noah's ark had been spotted somewhere near Mt. Ararat in modern times. Similarly the fact that pagan legend was said to contain accounts of a great flood, seemed in some way to backup the Bible record.

For the same reason it was interesting to learn from my mother that a non-Christian historian, Flavius Josephus, was quoted in the fourth century as recording information about "Jesus, a wise man". Mother gave me the tome to look at and I found myself reading it avidly at midday rest times. The relevant passage I found and which can be accessed on the Internet, is quoted by Eusebius in the fourth century:

Antiquities 18.3.3. *"Now there was about this time Jesus, a wise man, if it be lawful to call him a man, for he was a doer of wonderful works, a teacher of such men as receive the truth with pleasure. He drew over to him both many of the Jews, and many of the Gentiles. He was the Christ; and when Pilate, at the suggestion of the principal men amongst us, had condemned him to the cross, those that loved him at the first did not forsake him, for he appeared to them alive again the third day, as the divine prophets had foretold these and ten thousand other wonderful things concerning him; and the tribe of Christians, so named for him, are not extinct to this day"*

A rationalist taking a detached view of Christianity as judged by its historical effects on people and nations, would probably have to admit that, while debates and quarrels over its doctrine have caused immense damage to its own credibility and, at times, even been used as justification for violence, the civilising behaviour and virtues extolled in Christianity have undoubtedly been a powerful influence for good in all walks of life.

Countries in which Christian standards, as distinct from doctrinal bigotry, have historically been upheld, are often associated with material progress, respect and reliability.

In fact, a case could be made for Christianity's major role in the development of trust, the contract and work ethic, which have clearly created a climate for enterprise and endeavour.

Even an atheist must surely agree that Africa would be a more civilised and orderly continent than it is in the 21st century if its people had paid more attention to and adopted the values taught by Christian missionaries.

Remembering aspects of Mother's life in the context of faith and worship would be incomplete without some record of Chavuma in church.

In her Annual Chavuma report of 1934, Mother details: *"Ten meetings are held weekly on the station. It is very nice to see over 250 gathered for prayer in our weekly prayer meeting. Attendance at general services throughout the year averaged 325. Our plan is to be two months on the station and one in distant villages. Eleven distant villages have been visited this year and 15 000 natives reached".*

As indicated, missionaries were conscious of the danger that attention to the thriving work going on visibly at the station itself, might easily result in the remotely located heathen being neglected. In addition to the incursions into the untouched wilder areas, periodically a conference would be held at Chavuma, which included a feast as an incentive for attendance. Cattle were slaughtered and appetising food was cooked in large metal drums.

At the Chavuma communion service those ‘in fellowship’ sat in rows of pews forming a rectangle with each side facing the elements on a centre table. Because cash was not much in circulation and gifts in kind were common, the receptacles for offerings would have seemed unusual to new missionaries.

Two wooden receptacles with a handle on each end and a compartment for eggs and another for coins, were passed around. These items were products of the Chavuma carpentry shop, which under the skilled control of Wallace Logan produced so much useful equipment.

Manioc meal in a neat woven basket was a very common gift. Baskets would be placed on the floor next to the central table. Sometimes additional eggs would be pushed into the meal in the basket or placed on the table.

Mother who enjoyed humour like any other healthy well-adjusted person, told us of a missionary speaking at a report-back meeting in England, who said: “It’s so nice to see a native lady go up and lay an egg on the table”.

Another common gift was a live chicken placed with its legs tied alongside the baskets of meal. This miniature harvest festival was a weekly occurrence and the food was useful in feeding the refugees from witchcraft and for other mission needs.

One Sunday during the solemn service, Walter and I spotted a rather rebellious chicken that had decided not to take this treatment lying down. The burgeoning crown identified this young fowl as having potential to be cock-of-the walk should he survive this ordeal. Intelligently, this truly free-range specimen from a native village, pecked away at the string that hobbled him. Eventually under the transfixed eyes of two M.K’s, the sacrificial prisoner freed his legs and rose rather stiffly to his feet.

Enjoying the freedom, he emitted a loud triumphant squawk which alerted the congregation to the dreadful situation. Next he embarked on an excursion which really 'fowled' things up.

Looking for a better vantage point he took off and landed on the back rest of one of the pews just behind a worshipper. He silently surveyed the unfamiliar environment. Not another fowl in sight and a distinct lack of edible snippets around. Hold on, what was that on the table.
The M.K.'s were almost chortling aloud by now and then they noticed that a worthy female congregant strategically placed in the pew behind the escaped bird, was planning to do something about this disorderly behaviour. She leaned forward very slowly stalking the culprit.

With a lunge worthy of a charging lion, the lady grabbed a fist-full of handsome tail feathers and the screeching fowl flapped his wings wildly, taking him on a flight path directly to, but safely and mercifully, over the table and through the bars of an outside window to freedom.

The Lwena hymn book *Mukanda wa Myaso,* was a collection of hymns translated by the missionaries mostly from Sacred Songs and Solos and Golden Bells.

For example, Hymn No 159 gives the English title "Standing by a purpose true" and the tune is indicated as "Old S.S 7: New G.B 510".

The well-known chorus of the hymn, "Dare to be a Daniel" *(Ndanyele)* was translated as :

Umika mukwetu

Kava Ndanyele
Na Mucima wove wose
Fwelela Yesu

Literally this conveyed:
Be courageous my friend. Follow

the example of Daniel.
Like him, with all your heart,
Believe in Jesus.

156 *"O Love that will not let me go."*
S.S.S. 633

1 Zangi yove, Kalunga kami,
Ka yexi ku ngu sezako;
Hosena yi li na yami,
Ngu mwanove ngu na tokwa
Ca ku hambakana.

2 Zangi yove, Kalunga kami,
Yi na soloka ku ku fwa
Ca Mwanove a ci mwene
Mangana a ngu yoyese
Ami ngwa payile.

3 Zangi yove, Kalunga kami,
Yeji ku ngu pandamisa
Kuli Yove Muka-mwilu,
Ami ngwa sosolokele
Kwa ku sukusuku.

4 Zangi yove, Kalunga kami,
Ngu yivwenga mu mucima,
Ngu pwenga nawa na zangi
Kuli Yove wa livanga
Ku ngu zanga ami.

1

Page of the Lwena Hymn Book

Perhaps a slight historical misalignment for the Old Testament Daniel, but the evangelical message was more important than historical consistency. The fourth verse does introduce *Yehova Kalunga* (Jehova God) thereby perhaps mitigating what, in human terms, might be an anachronism.

The word *Kalunga* is interesting because while Daniel and many other Biblical characters had to be content with an Africanised English name, the Almighty already had a name among the African heathen and one which the missionary linguists such as Gavin Mowat and Albert Horton found acceptable as a label for the Christian God.

Natives learned the hymn tunes very quickly and harmonised pleasingly, except when the last note, usually a major tonic chord in Western hymns, was subjugated to the traditional native minor chord as described in an earlier chapter.

Since there was usually at least one missionary who knew the tune to any hymn, the congregation did not really need a musical instrument to lead the singing.

At worship services most of the Brethren tended to avoid using an organ or piano on the grounds that praise should not need any artificial enhancement. This seemed strange in the light of biblical injunctions such as that in Psalm 33: "Praise the Lord with the harp: sing unto Him with the psaltery and an instrument of ten strings".

Occasionally, therefore, without the guidance afforded by an organ or piano, the melody itself underwent a measure of evolution which no amount of vocal effort on the part of a purist songster among the missionaries seemed able to correct.

Both on the mission field and in Brethren assemblies at large, the risk existed that a wrong tune might be selected which fitted, say, the first two lines but alas either tune or words ran out so that extemporaneous melody adjustment or word repetition was required to finish the stanza. Once in a while a whole chorus or refrain of melody had to be sacrificed for lack of words.

The nature of the problem and its often amusing solution is illustrated in the factual instance where the first line of the hymn was:
"Before thy throne we bow", but being short of words to fill the number of beats in the line of melody selected, the congregation resorted to

singing "Before thy throne we bow, wow wow".

This was funny in those days but nowadays one has only to switch on your television, radio or a compact disc to hear songs actually written in a way which requires the singer to voice one vowel for as many as ten beats resulting in a yelling or howling effect that seemingly rakes in the royalties.

For as long as my brother and I could remember, Gladys Richards would appear on Sundays wearing a millinery delight in straw with a gargantuan fabric flower resting precariously on the wide brim. Her vibrato voice when singing seemed to resonate through her head so that the whole headdress tended to oscillate up and down with the gaudy flower flapping wildly in unison.

Diversions like that made the hard church seats easier for young boys to endure and somehow made the tedious hours pass more quickly.

What we have said about the paucity of shops, placed some severe limitations on how far a convert might shift to Western clothing. The main source of this style was cast-offs from missionaries. In many cases such clothing was already a cast-off when the missionary received it. There was another problem. The native recipient did not always know the purpose of a specific garment.

This provided even more amusement at services than Gladys Richard's floppy hat. Any newly acquired garment was automatically regarded as "Sunday best" dress and the most impressive venue to flaunt such *avant garde* apparel was the Chavuma assembly hall. Considerations of fit, match and appropriateness, even supposing they were understood, were not going to deter the owner from parading a heaven-sent and therefore rare creation.

We had seen flamboyant neck ties used as belts around the waist keeping up a pair of trousers that had seen better days and more than one owner.

Odd shoes were not uncommon nor were bulging skirts, better suited to someone half the size. Walter and I used to speculate about which missionary or M.K. had been the former owner.

One Sunday our glee knew no bounds when a dignified member from a nearby village strolled down the centre aisle in measured steps aimed at giving every fashion connoisseur a view of his new treasure. He was wearing a pair of perfect fitting striped pyjamas.

Since there was then only one male missionary at Chavuma, we knew we were looking at what Uncle Wallace Logan used to wear when retiring under his mosquito net.

Faith and superstition did not comfortably coexist, but except for the anger of the divining fraternity whose vested interests and power were eroded by Christian teaching, the conflict was largely spiritual. The visible evidence of conversion implied in discarding the magic charms, idols and trappings of African paganism, serving to make the new birth more dramatic and decisive. "Backsliding" was of course always a possibility, but few confessed conversion lightly, since crossing the floor meant facing castigation from those opposed, not to mention annoying the ancestors.

8. Hazards of the Wild

The reader will have become aware by now of some of the serious dangers and threats from both wild and human life.

Just as the 'glorious river' traverses rocky rapids where frightening jagged jaws jut above the tumbling surface causing the flow to break up into many faster moving flows, and hidden hazards lurking deeper pose a threat to any barge or canoe, so in my mother's experience unexpected threats to life and limb were ever present.

In this chapter are recounted more instances illustrating the adventurous and hazardous nature of the environment in which Mother and her family lived.

The taking daily of quinine tablets to fortify one against the insidious malaria and black water fever was a constant reminder of the threat from the female anopheles mosquito. Not only did we all suffer from serious malaria attacks despite the medicine, but our hearing became affected in later life from the constant doses of quinine. The more effective treatments now available had not yet been discovered. The well watered Balovale district was known for its malaria plague.

Another natural risk was that of sunstroke. Most missionaries wore the familiar headgear that became an icon of the African explorer-missionary, a helmet made of cork or pith. Even that formidable shield required a red sash to hang down the back of the neck for further protection. Those without helmets wore large brimmed hats together with the red sash, fixed to the hat by an elastic tape which did not take long to perish in the tropical climate.

I recall Grace, the youngest of the Logan girls, saying to the amusement of everyone: “mummy my last kick’s gone”.

Sunstroke was not a threat to be taken lightly. A young missionary, mentioned elsewhere in the narrative who worked tirelessly for long hours in the sun both in preaching and practical work such as making barges for river transport at Balovale, was eventually struck down by this terror. He experienced all the symptoms of delusion and nervous breakdown eventually being forced to leave the tropics.

He had been hearing heathen drumming in a nearby village, that no one else could hear. Moreover the drumming, he said, was a ritual linking him romantically to a native lass working on the station. This embarrassing delusion resulted in the sick man together with a senior missionary, walking miles through the hot sun to village after village without finding any dancing going on.

Against his will he had to be transported south for expert attention and care.

Africa is known for its venomous snakes. Snakes usually slithered away but presented a danger when aroused. Walter and I played with small harmless green grass snakes we found on the veranda.

There was a one metre drop from our veranda to the garden area. The veranda had a fence along its length of criss-crossed bamboo topped by a horizontal pole fixed between each upright and aesthetically encased in bamboo. As a two year old I was slumbering one afternoon in a hammock slung between two uprights holding the roof.
The hammock hung just above the level of the fence cross poles, to take advantage of the light breeze. My father just happened to look out of the lounge window and to his horror, saw an African cobra moving along the bamboo covered cross pole towards the hammock and beginning to rear its blown up hood in the classic striking position.

Fred reached for his double-barrelled shot gun which was resting on two pegs in the wall near the window. He had seconds in which to make a judgement as to whether the likely spread of the shot would endanger his son, then fired a shot killing the reptile which fell to the veranda floor beneath the hammock. Young Kapalu awoke unaware of the danger he had just escaped.

One evening returning in the dark from supper at the home of other missionaries, I felt something wrapping itself around my legs. Mother shone the hurricane lamp downwards and discovered it was a snake. She grabbed the nearest weapon, a piece of stiff string, doubled it and struck the snake till it lay writhing on the stone floor.

On another occasion Mother passed by the window of the bedroom in which Walter and I slept. Seeing a long snake with its head already through the window, its body vertical against wall and its tail stretched out on the floor, she took hold of the family pram, used by Dorothy and Margaret at the time, and pushed it backwards and forwards over the snake which became entangled in the spokes until it ceased moving.

The black spitting cobra, *Naja nigricollis,* when cornered will spit large quantities of venom over a distance of two metres. As described elsewhere, one of the native workers lifting huge stones at the front of our house to improve the depth of soil for a garden, received some cobra venom in his face. Only a little of the venom entered the man's eyes so the treatment by my mother prevented permanent blindness.

A midday rest hour, was mandatory at boarding school too. One rest hour, as we read books on our beds in the dormitory, a spitting cobra slithered up beside the bed on which John Faulkener, a contemporary M.K., was reading his book lying face downwards with his chin resting on his hands.

The creature spat venom which landed on the pages of the open book. I remember John springing up and shouting. The cobra took fright and made for a hole in the wall behind our clothes cupboard. Having disappeared into the hole there was now the risk that the snake would reappear after dark while we slept. If I recall correctly the hole was sealed, hopefully incarcerating the reptile permanently.

We loved boating in a dugout canoe on the Sakeji river, our twice weekly swimming venue at boarding school. One day after heavy rains when many creatures had been displaced by the high flood level, three of us we were paddling our canoe at speed down the strong flood current and suddenly what was probably a mamba, one of Africa's most venomous snakes, shot out of the trees, whose branches were partly submerged by the rushing river, and chased the canoe as we redoubled our paddling efforts eventually speeding to safety.

Among the curios Mother shipped to Melbourne in 1937, was a large python skin, peeled from a specimen caught near Chavuma hill.

At Chavuma just across the path from the Logan's house there was a small cave which opened into the side of the rocky hill and which also had a chimney-like vertical opening. At dusk we could see hundreds of bats flying in and out of the chimney. Sometimes we entered the cave from the larger opening to see the bats suspended upside-down from the cave ceiling. The pungent smell of bat droppings assailed our nostrils. On one occasion just as we were about to enter the cave we spotted a snake stretching its erect body and striking at the hanging bats.

An interesting place to find and catch bats was in the trumpet shaped fold of an, as yet, unfurled new leaf of the banana palm. We would block the open end of the trumpet with our hands and then slide our fingers upwards, pushing a soft lump towards the blocked open end. Inevitably the lump turned out to be a frightened bat who was glad to be released into the open air.

The variety of ants in tropical Africa is amazing; some of them quite dangerous.

The red army ants, *Eciton burchelli,* also known as Africa soldier or driver ants, are voracious predators. They cling tightly to one another (in large groups of 10,000 to 500,000) as they travel across land and water looking for food and attacking any animals that get in their path. These vicious creatures have been known to kill tarantulas, lizards, birds, snakes, pigs and sometimes animals as large as antelope.

Walter and I loved keeping pets such as rabbits, guinea pigs, birds and other small creatures. Young natives would often sell a wild canary in a beautifully made bamboo and grass cage of about 20 cubic centimetres. Normally these cages had a top deck which could be used as a trap to catch other canaries. The singing of the captive bird together with some bird seed, *masangu,* would attract a free canary whose arrival would collapse the open lid, capturing it.

At one time we successfully kept seven wild canaries, *patalo,* in a large cage. They gave much pleasure with their rich and melodious song. The family went on a three day village campaign leaving the canaries under the care of the house maid. On our return we found the house overrun with red army ants consuming every edible substance in sight and only the cleaned bones of canaries lying at the bottom of their cage.

The house maid survived the ants but not the wrath of the M.K.'s

White ants, which are, strictly speaking, termites *(isoptera),* abound in tropical Africa. Their well structured and disciplined life as a colony of workers, soldiers, reproducers and other specialised functionaries, is an example of order that the indigenous humans in the continent seemed to have neglected.

Chavuma hill was surrounded by anthills often two metres high. The clay from these mounds was useful in building the paths on the mission station. Seasonally those members of a colony that grew wings, would emerge from the anthill in their hundreds on, what is known as, the honeymoon flight. Those that escaped hungry birds and bats landed, cast their wings and proceeded to search for a mate with whom to dig into soil or wood starting a new colony.

Their eating habits presented a serious problem. Houses built of poles and mud often collapsed because the white ants had eaten out the inside of the poles often making clay tunnel-like walkways up into the timber.

Even in brick houses ant-proof coursing of galvanised metal sheeting, was frequently used between two of the lower rows of bricks, with a protruding edge bent down to discourage these foragers. Food left on the ground almost anywhere, risked their grateful and swift appearance.

On one journey to school we were accompanied by Samuel Arnot, whose parents worked at Kalunda in Angola. Inside the tent we slept on a canvas sheet thrown on the ground.

Samuel had been chewing on some raw manioc root. It was probably some residue of the poisonous outer layer that made him sick that night. During the night he vomited on the tent floor, considerately, just off the canvas sheet, and then went off to sleep. In the morning we woke to find the termites had come to the surface cleaned up all the mess and had aerated Samuel's underclothing left on the bare ground, making it look for all the world like the nearest thing to a pair of fashion lace panties you could find in that part of the world.

The white ants' habit of vibrating their heads on the ground in unison, when disturbed was a strange phenomenon.

Every time you stamped your foot the ants would spontaneously respond with the sound of a thousand vibrating heads, stopping abruptly like a well-trained orchestra. The effect was highlighted when the army was devouring paper left on the ground since the vibration of heads resonated more audibly against paper.

Some missionaries believed there was nothing these insects weren't prepared to eat. Certain species can apparently digest even cellulose.

I recall Mother opening up the Chavuma house of a single missionary, Irma Motter, who had been away in Canada for a while, and finding virtually all fabrics and furniture either in tatters or consumed by termites.

The stark scene included a gramophone of which all the leather casing had been devoured and the metal parts lay forlornly on the ground. But even the chromium plated metal showed signs of a rusty encrustation. A cabinet of cutlery had been treated with similar dispatch and to our amazement one high quality table knife had a hole, apparently actually eaten, right through the blade.

Walter, who later became an internationally renowned expert on corrosion, explains that termites deposit ascetic acid (vinegar) which being an aggressively corrosive agent can destroy even chrome-plated metal.

Perhaps the fact that white ants were an edible delicacy, afforded a way of taking revenge on these destructive insects. Natives used to place a woven conically shaped sifting basket over the part of the anthill from which the honeymooners were emerging. This would collect hundreds of flying ants who quickly discarded their wings and were then harvested as food.

M.K.'s used to catch a few and roast them over a paraffin lamp probably more for bravado than real enjoyment. I found that as long as you kept the loose wings out of your mouth, flying ants were as tasty as a morsel of spiced chicken.

The exotic moths have already been mentioned. In their caterpillar state, some species were quite horrifying. Climbing one of central Africa's lovely trees once, I felt a sharp stab of pain in my leg. I had been pricked by a brightly coloured yellow and green caterpillar, with a ridge of sharp orange-tinged spines. A septic sore developed from the venom discharged, leaving a lifetime scar. This was probably the stinging caterpillar, *sibine stimulea.*

On the banks of the Sakeji River at the missionary boarding school, one M.K., Stephen Fisher, a great tree climber, collected some bristles in his hand after touching a huge caterpillar.

We gathered round and soon spotted the giant crawler, greyish in colour and very hairy.

Headmaster Nightingale did an uncharacteristic thing. Whether interested from an entomological point of view or just wanting to rid the play area of the pest, he did not explain. Climbing the tree he pulled himself along the overhanging branch, hand-over-hand with his face turned upwards towards the 15 centimetre prickler. The caterpillar suddenly shot a jet of inky black solution directly at his face. The liquid spread all over his glasses which he was fortunately wearing. He let go of the branch and dropped to the ground as quickly as Stephen had done.

The big cats were never far away. Many a time while travelling in the bush we would come within a few metres of a lion and stand still until, after a searching stare, the king of the beasts went on his way.

Travelling down the Zambezi we would often, from the safety of the barge, see a pride at the river's edge quenching its collective thirst.

In a letter on 25th August 1941, Wallace Logan described some experiences of the very earliest motor travel near Chavuma.

"...animals of all kinds crossed our path. Three nights in succession lions came within 3 feet of our tent. We also had to beat out bush fires".

Danger came even closer to home at times. One late afternoon we were playing around our home and Mother was applying a solution of permanganate of potash, to a native bitten by a snake, when we heard a yelp from our watchdog. Rushing around to that side of the house, there was no sign of the poor canine though the leopard's spoor in the sand was

Gavin, Mother and Walter with leopard trapped and shot

only too clear.

Leopards were very common especially around the Arnot's station, Kalunda, Angola. We were staying with them overnight on one of our trips to school when their dog gave a pitiful yelp as it was taken by a leopard off the veranda.

When carnivores get too old to hunt with the pride in the normal way, sheep and goats from the native villages provide an alternative way to survive, securing meat without having to stalk and chase it. Villagers too, were occasional victims.

A leopard had been decimating the sheep and goats from a village near Chavuma and the inhabitants had prevailed upon Wallace Logan to lend them a bear trap. One day a runner arrived with news of success. *"Mwata, Mwata"* he shouted, "the leopard is trapped!".

Wallace grabbed a rifle and jumping on his motor cycle, then the only motorised form of transport at Chavuma, rode out to the village. On arrival he could see a large crowd which had formed a circle around the leopard who was straining to release a rear leg from the trap and roaring ferociously at the crowd. Every time he charged forward the chain fixing the trap to a stout tree stretched taut and the pain in the leopard's leg infuriated him all the more.

Logan noticed that the leopard's violent tugging seemed to have broken the bone at the point where the trap held the leg. This angry leopard was on the point of breaking free and wreaking havoc on the unsuspecting crowd. Without delay Logan felled the leopard with a single shot. Going up to inspect the beautiful animal he found that only a piece of its beautiful hide and a few tendons, remained holding the leopard in the trap. The timing of that shot had almost certainly saved the lives of more than one villager.

When Stanley Arnot of Kalunda was a baby, sleeping in a cot inside the camp tent, a lion actually entered the tent, took the cot in his teeth and pulled it outside, baby and all. The baby's father Nigel, was awakened by the commotion and shouted for the porters who brandished flaming torches taken from the camp fire and frightened the lion off. Baby Stanley was unharmed.

The blood curdling sound of a hungry hyena could be heard almost anywhere shortly after sunset. Although they tended to prowl behind the big cats to scavenge pickings, occasionally humans would be attacked.

In one of Mother's letters she writes of "a little girl brought to the hill, having been badly mauled by a hyena". I recall that the hyena had entered a native hut in a village across the river from Chavuma. The doorway had only a stiff straw mat laid across it mainly to keep out chickens and goats. On raising the alarm, the child's father and other villagers had chased the hyena off by brandishing flaming wood from among the embers of the village fire.

Apart from the severe wounds inflicted by the hyena's powerful jaw, its diet of carrion renders its teeth highly likely to result in sepsis especially in the tropical climate.

Travelling by barge up the Zambezi in the Angolan stretch of the river, we once caught sight of freshly stripped leaves and branches floating down the river. The paddlers said there were elephants near. Soon we became aware of the strong smell of a herd and swarms of flies everywhere. Suddenly around the next river bend we spotted a large herd of these African giants crossing the river which at that point, just south of Kazombo, was narrow enough to make this feasible.

The barge was pulled to one side and kept stationary in the water until the noisy trumpeting giants had gone on their way.

In the dry season elephants often made pests of themselves to villagers by invading the meagre manioc and maize fields and devouring precious sustenance. The flaming torch defence did not always work and from time to time villagers were trampled to death by a herd of hungry and angry elephants.

Certain plants were dangerous. At Chavuma we had hedges of the *Lunana* cactus which when broken, exuded a milk which was extremely painful if accidentally placed in the eye and reputed to potentially cause blindness. One day Walter and I had been digging below a *lunana* hedge and suddenly our eyes became very painful. Our hands had picked up some of the sticky milk from the *lunana* roots which had then been rubbed into our eyes. It took Mother some considerable time and effort to provide relief.

In addition to the hookworm threat, there were a number of diseases which could be caught walking barefoot, such as the jigger flea *(Sarcopsylla penetrans)* which usually got into a toe, burrowing and creating a nodule full of whitish matter.

The uncomfortable itching and annoying pain could be stopped only when a skilled nurse took out the whole nodule taking care not to burst it thereby spreading the 'eggs'. The jigger flea apparently came from Rio de Janeiro via Angola and quickly spread through tropical Africa.

Incidentally research suggests that the rather coarse term "I'll be jiggered" comes from British sailors in the tropics who acquired these pesky critters, especially under their toenails.

Dangers ranged from furious hornets to angry hippos; from poisonous caterpillars to voracious crocodiles and from stinging scorpions to venomous snakes. Life was a constant adventure.

9. *Chavuma's Children*

The great Zambezi frequently formed separate streams and branches spreading its life-giving waters more generously.

Geographical evidence of a river's age is provided by the occasional semi-circular lake alongside the main stream, especially in flatter areas. These lakes represent former curves in the river course which had been cut through by flood torrents in the rainy season, when the speed and volume of the river demanded a short cut.

Both the formation of curves and the short cuts leaving semicircular lakes close to each bank, are part of a cycle of known river behaviour and have a scientific explanation involving the amount of silt dropped by the water at varying speeds of flow.

The effect of these riverine characteristics, is to share and distribute the water supply beyond the banks of the mainstream.

And so, allegorically, the glorious river again symbolises my mother's principled and unselfish life and her capacity for benevolence, for sharing and sustaining others.

This is inescapable to the Children of Chavuma. But not only were I and my siblings the beneficiaries of Mother's influence, our playmates in the Logan family have given testimony to their impressions of her caring and cheerful influence.

The four of us were exceedingly fortunate to have a mother who did not constantly bemoan her fate having to play the role of father, mother, nurse and then teacher.

The usual colds, measles and whooping cough and of course malaria, jigger fleas and a host of tropical ailments all had to be attended to.

We were far from saintly in any special way, so guidance as well as discipline was required. The odd scrape or bite, mischief and naughtiness, tears and laughter were our lot. Perhaps being so close to nature and danger yet looking to a parent, who did experience anxiety but handed it all on to the One who had sent her there, helped to make us stronger.

Dorothy and Margaret were identical twins so alike that even Mother had ribbon tied around Dorothy's ankle when they were born. Even while developing individual characters they remained look-alikes.

The tip of Margaret's nose was very slightly flatter than her sister's. Mother had mentioned that the nose was the same shape as that of Margaret's grand aunt Louie.

As teasing brothers, Walter and I, maintained that an aeroplane could land on Margaret's nose, (though we had seen an aircraft only in pictures).

The twins took our teasing in good spirit as they did the tricks we used to play on them.

Sometimes the rest hour, compulsory in the tropics, became an occasion for dramatic presentations put on by the brothers for the benefit of the twins. Disguising ourselves as visitors from another planet we would perform many weird antics of magic.

One of these dramatic scenes was curiously like the raising of the deceased prophet Samuel, by the witch at Endor (I Samuel 28).

Kapalu, Moni and Kaumba

The twins soon showed musical talent singing sweetly under Mother's tutorship and playing the organ.

Walter and I had a young native friend who, in addition to kitchen duties, was retained to keep us out of mischief while Mother was at work. His name was Moni.

Moni taught us a little bush craft. We learnt the Lwena names for birds, snakes or other creatures we came across as we walked around Chavuma hill; the difference between indigenous shrubs, how to blow a loud shrill whistle by putting your thumbs together and blowing on a blade of grass placed between them. We learnt to make a realistic dove call, to make a catapult from a twig of the right shrub and how to use it skilfully.

To satisfy our curiosity about the inverted cone-shaped pits to be found in the soft dry sand under house eaves or other shelter, Moni demonstrated the ways of the amazing ant lion by dropping a small black ant into the pit. We watched the ant struggling to escape up the steep and unstable slope, suddenly the ant lion's piercing mandibles emerged from under the sand and drew the victim under, to be devoured out of sight.

Should the struggling ant manage to stick desperately to the sides of the pit, the crafty ant lion would send a shower of sand flying up to knock his prey down to certain death. After the meal, the ant lion would clean out his home by ejecting the carcass and other debris restoring the smooth and lethal slopes of his perfect trap.

Moni was very interested in learning the ways of the white man. Having picked up a smattering of English and some spelling, while performing kitchen duties for Mother, he had become intrigued by the words 'made in England' which appeared on so many items we had around the house. Mother had explained the usage to him. One day after he had shaken the tin of buttermilk sufficiently to churn it into homemade butter, he formed the butter into a cube on a dish and inscribed on it the words "made in Moni".

We loved walking around in the nearby bush with our catapults. Best of all were the excursions down to the river on a steep and stony footpath through the forest. At the river, numerous small boys would appear as if from nowhere and help us to find worms to bait our hooks.

Back: Margaret, Mother, Dorothy
Front: Gavin, Walter at home

Often the hooks were merely bent pins, though as we grew older Mother managed to get us supplies of real fish-hooks with the vital barb. For rods we used a length of bamboo or a stick.

The sound of the river rushing by and the lapping of waves on the sandy shore made a great environment for two boys bent on hooking some unwary fish. The crocodile menace kept us firmly on the shore but the Zambezi's teaming fish always seemed willing to oblige.

At certain seasons of the year small fish would dig into the sand between stones and seemed to hibernate in preparation for the lowering of the water level in the dry season, during which the dampness of the sand apparently provided sufficient water for survival. Our young native friends showed us how to extricate these fish from their hiding places a metre or so above the water line.

We usually had a pet or two to look after. The natives were always bringing some small animal or bird to sell for sixpence or a shilling. Tortoises, monkeys and birds were among the many pets we loved.

One little vervet monkey became so much a part of the household, he would sit at the table when we had tea. Mother made him a little red suit on the treadle sewing machine which he seemed quite happy to wear.

One day he put his hand out to the tea pot as Mother poured the tea and ran screeching away in pain. He enjoyed the fuss we made over him, happily submitting to having his burns treated including a bandage.

Sadly, one day, a housemaid, who disliked the monkey, took a box used for sifting sand having wire mesh on one of the open sides, and placed it over him on the veranda. She went off duty leaving him still trapped. A heavy storm came up soaking him. He died not long after.

Perhaps our most notable pet was Peter the mongrel. We first saw him as a small white puppy in a village in which we camped overnight. His handsome face and cute paws set him aside as superior to most of the canines we had seen in the villages. The owner, noting our interest offered the pup for sale to Mother. A price eventually agreed, Peter came home with us to Chavuma. Considering we had no veterinary service or anti-biliary inoculation, we were taking a risk.

Peter grew into a beautiful hound and gave us much joy for some years before he succumbed to disease and had to be put down. This was a euphemism for being led away some distance, supposed to be out of earshot, and felled by a shot from a musket. The executioner ignored our instructions and it was a sad and cruel experience for us to hear the fatal shot and his pathetic yelp.

The Logan Family

Before Peter's arrival, a wild dog would occasionally find it convenient to spend the night in a box of papers and toys on our veranda.

The prevalence of rabies and the risk of bubonic plague from fleas made this undesirable. Without risking a fatal bite it was difficult to discourage the scrawny cur. Walter and I erected a platform of stones above the box, held in position by an upright stake which rested on a flimsy base. That night from the safety of our bedroom we expectantly and, I suppose, rather cruelly awaited the arrival of the regular nocturnal visitor. Soon we heard him climb into the box. The stake was dislodged and the platform tumbled down upon this hapless version of man's best friend. The trick worked - we had no more visits.

The Barnett four grew up alongside the Logan seven. In many ways, I suppose, Wallace Logan became what psychologists would call a father figure, in the absence of our own father. Certainly there was always a supportive and loving relationship between the two families.

The eldest Logan girls, twins Frances and Esther were away at school in our early years and Grace, Paul and David were closer to my twin sisters in age. For Walter and I, being very close in age, Eleanor and Viola were our opposite numbers as it were.

What lovely girls they all turned out to be - really quite beautiful. When Walter and I saw them as adults many years later we were astonished at how much we had taken them for granted as children.

I remember a native *nduna* at a village campfire meeting remarking that Esther and Francis were beautiful. Mrs. Logan immediately pointed out to the gathering that it was the inner beauty that came with salvation and not nature's endowments that really mattered.

The Logan children faithfully followed their parents in missionary careers. Some of them working at Chavuma and others establishing new stations in the region.

While writing this book, I tried to make contact with Eleanor and to my delight managed to discover an e-mail address and had the happy experience of receiving a message from John and Eleanor Sims while they were in the USA, but planning to go back to their chosen missionary field in stricken and dangerous Zimbabwe. Eleanor provided some useful insight into my mother's life as recorded in this chronicle.

John, the lucky man Eleanor married, was the son of Chavuma pioneers Mr. and Mrs. Bert Sims.

When Walter and I were about four and five respectively, Bert Sims paid a visit to Chavuma and my special memory of him was teaching us to stand to attention and salute smartly when he blew a whistle.

As small children Walter and I often played happily with Eleanor and Viola. We were really like brothers and sisters.

Eleanor was a little ahead of all of us on what one might call awareness, and once initiated reading or looking at books under blankets on a couch in the Logan's lounge. The giggling that went on when toes touched and tickled, drew Mrs Logan's attention to the debauchery and, lifting the blanket she administered a punishing slap to all legs which could remotely be said to be in a compromising position.

This did not rule out more secretive meetings away from the Logan house where the inevitable "I'll show you mine" type of learning curve, took its natural course. Neither Viola (now deceased) nor Eleanor, who both later became such a lovely missionary ladies and married two fine young missionaries, are likely to feel libelled by this revelation.

One afternoon Eleanor and I walked through some of rooms at the rear of the church hall with its neat thatched roof, no ceilings and solid timber doors produced in the station carpentry shop.

We had been in one room awhile and Eleanor announced that she could not open the door. I cannot remember whether or not I tried to open it. We decided that eventually someone would come looking for us. It was a long time before we were missed and eventually an elder, Sapindalo, came and opened the door from outside apparently without any problem.

As I recall Mother and Ruth Logan had some discussion about whether or not Eleanor and I had planned to get ourselves 'lost'. We both enjoyed being lost and found and seemed, in due course, to have been given the benefit of the doubt.

A few years later Walter and I had not only become shy of girls but were displaying the normal scorn for them that boys seem to pretend, probably in suppression of their natural curiosity.

Because Sakeji School was two weeks journey there and another fortnight back, joint parental efforts were made to teach us the three R's at home so as to delay the inevitable need to travel to formal school. Mother and a Canadian single missionary Irma Motter, held regular classes for Chavuma's children with some assistance from Mrs Ruth Logan.

By the time Eleanor and I, at seven, began formal schooling, we were already reading and writing competently and had a basic knowledge of arithmetic.

Some years later, Frances and Esther who had completed the education available from Sakeji School, were doing some home learning courses and regularly got us all involved in various projects. The Logans were very artistic and showed us techniques with water colours that went beyond what we all learned at Sakeji.

"Spatograph" was the name they gave to rubbing a toothbrush in paint and brushing it against a piece of wire mesh, so that spats of paint would fall evenly on the art work except for any portion over which a template had been placed.

The template might be some fancy lettering or a flower so that the unspotted part of the work would profile the object.

The Barnett children were themselves fairly artistic and we painted many a bible text on scrolls using Old English text style lettering. We became adept at adding shading and sometimes we cut out the capital letters placing brightly coloured chocolate paper behind.

The Logan's with their greater material resources, not to mention their natural creativity and initiative, organised many absorbing hours for all of us.

Of course we boys did not appreciate it all, at the time. This was especially true of a bible study type project which Frances and Esther launched, called the P.S.G. There was homework involved and other activities which we thought were infantile or girlish. While I cannot recall what the acronym P.S.G. actually stood for, I do remember that Walter and I used, in private, to refer to the venture as the Pig's Society of Gibberish. I feel ashamed now at this indication of ingratitude.

Wallace Logan's carpentry shop was always an intriguing place for Walter and I. The sound of the hand saw and the plane or spoke shave, the smell of fresh saw-dust and shavings, the soft feel of shavings under foot, the stocks of locally cured timber and the large workbench, all combined in an exciting world of industry.

The old dark store-house behind our home, already referred to, was another interesting place to explore when Mother occasionally opened it up. We would be close behind her, peering with the aid of torch light into the musty rooms, at the bags of peanuts and manioc meal, chasing a frantic rat or two dashing into a dark corner and charmed by a cat with a family of newly born and still blind kittens.

Mystery is always intriguing to boys and we were puzzled by a flashing light that some nights would appear on the hill opposite Chavuma. There was no village on that hill. The countryside was largely rough indigenous bush so that the presence of any reflective material was very unlikely. Our servants used to puzzle over the phenomenon. The natives often had a supernatural explanation for something like that.

At one stage two foreign prospectors had camped in the area assessing it for metal mining potential. In due course the prospectors moved away. Apparently they had concluded there was, so to speak, no 'ore inspiring' prospect in that region. The lights continued spasmodically after the prospectors had gone and no one ever solved the mystery.

After the outbreak of the Second World War, the colonial administration sent a contingent to train native soldiers and doubtless to keep an eye on the Angolan neighbours. The army camped on the west bank below the falls. Occasionally the officers would visit Chavuma mission for a social afternoon which would not be without its word from the good book and some singing. I recall meeting Paddy Miller on that occasion, a young man who had earlier been a Sakeji boy and had just been promoted to the military rank of captain.

Some of the military guests were in our home poring over Mother's large cloth map of central Africa. Locating Chavuma, attention was drawn to the straight east-west line of the Angolan boundary on the 13° latitude South. As related earlier, this boundary line had been the result of an arbitrary act of impulse on the part of Cecil Rhodes.

Our guests jokingly suggested that, since they were in the vicinity, it might give them a more tangible purpose for being there, were they to "re-annex" the stretch of the Zambezi which Rhodes had so thoughtlessly given away. It would also make the map neater, they felt.

Though spoken jokingly, I suppose these sentiments quoted in modern politically correct company, might add fuel to the proverbial fire of anti-colonial and anti-imperialist invective so popular in Africa today.

A reciprocal visit was paid to the army camp, where we saw our first example of marching in step under the command of a sergeant major. Amusingly I recall the tent temporarily erected as a pantry for food supplies. At one side a crude table had been placed at which sat a uniformed man examining and purchasing produce proffered by the locals including eggs, fowls, vegetables and milk. As each deal was done, cash was paid and the seller told to go around to the rear of the tent and deposit the goods on tables provided. It did not take the locals too long to tumble to the fact that, since no one was checking delivery behind the pantry, one could sell the same goods over again.

By the time the British army discovered this chicanery, some crafty vendors had managed to sell their wares up to four times. Perhaps the missionary influence was not as strong on that remote side of the river.

Death had made its way into my consciousness quite early from the gospel tenet that dying without spiritual regeneration meant eternal damnation. Death had in a very personal way impacted my mother and deprived me of a father.

Though I was aware that funerals were for farewells and burials, it was nevertheless a shock, at a funeral service on the slopes of Chavuma hill, when running from my seat, to trip over human feet protruding from a bundle of saplings and sticks which bound a body and served as a coffin.

Somehow all the familiar references to the soul being "absent from the body" and wafted into eternity, left me unprepared to encounter a dead body in this way.

I suppose if I'd stayed on my uncomfortable seat until the service was properly over and suppressed my desire to run around on such a solemn occasion, I might have been spared the ordeal.

Natives of our own age often taught us aspects of bush craft. Having seen them snaring village chickens almost as a practice run for game birds, we quickly learned how to make a trap using a young branch to which a string would be attached and the other end made into a noose. The string would be pulled down bending the flexible sapling into a spring. The noose would be opened, held down and spread open on the ground by cleverly positioning short sticks so that treading on them would release the string, the noose would close over the bird's leg and the freed sapling springing back, would tighten the noose, jerking the bird off the ground.

On one occasion we set up such a trap and chased one or two village chickens around a hut towards some tasty morsels scattered on the ground. Spotting the bait, the birds cooperated eagerly in the cruel plot which ended up with a squawking, flapping chicken dangling by a leg from the sprung sapling. This 'fowl' play afforded us much amusement until Mother decided otherwise.

The natives collected mushrooms which seasonally grew prolifically in forest areas. They knew which to avoid. Yet occasionally there were deaths from mushroom poisoning. Walter and I learned to recognise edible mushrooms and the family often enjoyed a tasty meal of these wild delights.

I particularly remember a large white-grey mushroom with a smooth skin and bulbous shape, a red-orange one called *uchila-chila* and a tasty light-brown variegated specimen.

One evening all Chavuma's children were dining at the Barnett's house while the adults were combining a business meeting with dinner at the Logans.

We had just begun to enjoy a meal of the light-brown mushrooms when a servant rushed in from the Logan's house with a message to stop eating the mushrooms as they were poisonous. Those of us who had already consumed a little, felt uneasy. One of the Logan girls reckoned she felt sick.

Our table boy had just arranged something less exotic when the same messenger rushed in to say the mushrooms were alright and that a mistake had been made. At this good news we all got stuck into the mushrooms except for the queasy one, and polished off the lot. After the meal was over the messenger rushed in a third time, to say that the mushrooms were poisonous after all.

Despite no stomach pumps or expert medical treatment, no one experienced any adverse consequences, not even the queasy one!

Growing up in a missionary family and among other M.K.'s, held the inherent risk of what I came to think of as the "receiver syndrome". Missionaries to darkest Africa were, in the nature of things, seen as heroic people deserving of all sorts of kindness and material support.

This was especially the case with Brethren missionaries whose survival depended totally on gifts. Although one's parents clearly worked extremely hard under exhausting and debilitating conditions, their children saw little connection between the work and the pay, as it were. The material sustenance arrived spasmodically with the postman, in contrast to the situation where workers collect their pay at regular working intervals. The postman was more like Father Christmas than the paymaster.

When mission folk visited us or we travelled through their areas, there was usually generous accommodation and often gifts of some kind or other. Children always got special treatment when it came to gifts. The situation was naturally heightened where the recipients were fatherless. Sympathy and generosity almost knew no bounds. This, however, is not to suggest that there was any luxury or abundance.

No wonder then, like many M.K.'s, we found ourselves expecting largess whenever visiting or visited. Going on furlough raised the syndrome to fever pitch. Would the nice uncle hand out some sweets or a toy? What would we get in the mail this time? The fact that we were supposed to see these gifts as coming from the hand of God, served to make the whole process eminently respectable.

Mother used to speak to us severely whenever she detected traits of the receiver syndrome in our attitude. We had no special rights and, gratitude not expectation, was the appropriate stance. The Bible, she pointed out, supported the work ethic. "If a man will not work neither shall he eat." Moreover "it is more blessed to give than to receive".

This latter quotation was to cause me some amusement years later when visiting the office of the Receiver of Revenue in Johannesburg. On the office wall of my tax assessor a motto read: "it is more blessed to give than to receive".

It is probably thanks to that sensible attitude among most missionaries, that M.K.'s from Sakeji School largely turned out to be responsible, industrious and successful adults generally unspoiled by the kindness and gifts of concerned people.

I often wonder whether Africa's well-known "receiver syndrome" might have been avoided, had the same attitude been taken by the world at large towards the continent's familiar begging bowl stance.

Walter showed his daring more than I did. He was quicker to get riding a bicycle and not afraid to crash. Crossing a river in an unsteady dugout was a terrifying ordeal for me.

Fear of failure often overcame me in such situations so that my performance itself was impaired. All I needed to set me crying like a baby was to be laughed at, having fallen off my bike or made an ass of myself in some way or other.

However, being something of a stage manager, I was ironically, sometimes not able to resist acting as a show-off, thereby frequently setting myself up for a showdown and the chagrin that would follow.

How privileged I was to have a mother who perceived these traits early and, instead of scorning me for them, helped one to look out in advance for situations in which one's weaknesses might be exposed.

In addition to constantly reiterating the gospel message of salvation to their own children, missionaries did of course pray often and earnestly for their salvation. It would be difficult in this atmosphere for any such child not to respond.

Since the new birth was a matter of exercising faith, one was not expected to feel any different other than relief at meeting a parental expectation and of course avoiding eternal punishment. A new parental expectation, namely to display the 'fruits of the spirit' and behave like a child of God, now became evident.

In the case of the heathen, there were many overt behaviours which changed or were expected to do so. In the conversion of a heathen murderer there is a dramatic repentance and overt change. For missionary children however, the new birth was almost inevitably an un-dramatic transition. Some could not tell you when they were 'saved'. Others could point to a critical incident such as a meeting at which a particularly emotional or striking appeal had been made following the preaching of eternal punishment, heightened perhaps by the poignant harmony and lyrics of a gospel hymn.

While the experience of baptism was, scripturally, no more than a public declaration of such response it was noticeable that some M.K.'s seemed to acquire an aura of saintliness after baptism.

No one ever mentioned observing anything approaching saintliness in my case, but both Walter and I observed this of our Logan contemporaries. I remember agreeing with Walter that Eleanor seemed to have become "more quiet and serious" after she was baptised.

In 1936 having reached the age of seven, it was time for this Child of Chavuma to go to boarding school. Mother had by then already done a good job of getting me literate and handy with figures.

Sakeji School for M.K.'s was a remarkable institution which avoided missionaries having to return to their land of origin for the sake of their children's education. A chapter in these chronicles is devoted to the school.

Sakeji was, even in the 1930's, relatively well served by roads, that is two parallel dirt tracks which were accessible to motor vehicles provided the fast growing tropical bush was kept at bay. Until the forties, Chavuma was not one of the places that could be reached by such roads.
Taking one's son to school was not just a walk down the road. This was two weeks journey on trek through rugged bush, crossing fast flowing rivers on a fallen tree trunk, encountering wild animals crossing the borders of another country, carrying enough non-perishable food and camping equipment in addition to clothing and medicines. Then there was the journey back, a month out of your life.

Of course Mother made each night's stop in a native village an opportunity to preach the gospel of good news to people who, far from any mission station, rarely heard it.

The Logan twins Frances and Esther had already attended Sakeji for a couple of years. Mother's safari party, on this my first journey to school, included Frances, Esther and Eleanor Logan also facing her first term, and the rest of the young Barnett family, too young to be left behind.

Thirty porters had been engaged. Thirty loads of 26 kilograms were weighed on a hanging scale and packed. These included the tent, its fly cover, a canvas bath, folding chairs and cooking utensils. There were two carriers for each hammock and a cook-boy. In all, this made for about 57 mouths to feed en route and a substantial number of unschooled people to manage.

Fresh water would be taken from the sparkling rivers and boiled to avoid bilharzia. Hopefully fresh milk could be purchased in villages visited on the journey.

Mother had selected the route through the Manyinga district, described in my father's letters quoted earlier. This was not the shortest route but it avoided entering Angola and aimed to bring us out near Mwinilunga where Sakeji's deputy principal Lyndon Hess was due to meet us in a leviathan called a Model T Ford.

We travelled in hammocks slung from a palm pole, with a covering of cloth and protective red fabric flaps which could be let down each side to help in the constant fight against sunstroke.

As described elsewhere, each bearer had one hand on the pole to keep it on his shoulder and in the other, waved a *mufuka*, a fly whisk, made from the tail of an antelope.

A typical day took us nearly 50 kilometres between camps, usually in or near a native village. Eating beside the log camp fire under the starry African sky, complaints and wounds would be attended to, the gospel service or Bible reading conducted and then we would settle down to sleep on folding camp beds snug inside the green canvas tent.

Breakfast was hot porridge boiled on the revived camp fire. A noonday stop for lunch near a rushing river provided a few moments to fling a

M.K.'s makeshift line at some rainbow coloured fish and enjoy a tin of canned baked beans or bully beef with the inevitable *shima.* These luxuries were forced on us since there was no way of preserving perishable food.

There was only one mission station on that route, namely Kamapanda. The senior missionaries there were Mr and Mrs Cunningham. Mr Cunningham used to enjoy telling us stories from the very earliest days at Kamapanda. On one occasion he had encountered a difficult and recalcitrant native chief whose refusal to cooperate was hindering the mission. He told the chief that unless he cooperated he would reluctantly have to use some of his persuasive powers. The chief asked for an example of such powers, whereupon Cunningham took out his set of false teeth and holding them menacingly in his hand, ran after the chief who bolted in fear, shouting his agreement to cooperate at once.

After two weeks moving along a narrow, barely visible footpath, the troop came across two parallel tracks with bush cut back a metre on each side and in between. This was the motor road, the first I had seen. It ended abruptly at our feet and ran forward in a more or less straight line disappearing into the thick jungle.

In an atmosphere of tension and some anxiety on my part, we prepared to wait for the arrival of Lyndon Hess, who would take us away from my mother in a curiosity known as a car, powered by a noisy, angry sounding internal combustion engine.

Sakeji was fortunate enough to have a cast-off Ford model T previously owned by ffolliat Fisher of Hillwood Farm.

Eventually in the late afternoon, the unfamiliar sound of a motor was heard approaching. As the car emerged from the bush, what I later learned were headlights, seemed to stare ominously. The tall and handsome Lyndon Hess emerged from this juggernaut and greetings took place.

My brother Walter was relaxed since he was not going to be press- ganged into the cage on wheels. He was not headed for, who knew what misery, at boarding school, - not that year anyway.

The parting was tearful and my cries rang through the forest until, to my mother's ears, fading eventually as the vehicle drove relentlessly onwards soon engulfed by the forest.

The Logan twins were amused at my torture having trod this way before. Eleanor was far braver than I and just kept a stiff upper lip. Soon the curiosity of moving in this noisy chariot and the speed with which the trees flashed past, served to distract and the rest of the passengers welcomed the silence. Even so, noticing Hess's eyes peering at me through the rear view mirror was a little unnerving.

Sakeji Class of 1936

Back Row: *Frank Horton, Esther Logan, Joyce Fisher, Violet Haile, Nan Hoyte, Francis Logan, Joan Hoyte, Cecil Haile*

Middle Row: *Irene Stevenson, Alice Horton, Ethel Stevenson, Peggy Fisher, Sheila Fisher, Wynn Nightingale, Nel Hoyte*

Front Row: *Lois Horton, John Faulkener, Chris Hoyte, Gavin Barnett, Audrey Prescott, Eleanor Logan, Anne Fisher*

10. Yambeji of Yesteryear

Mother had been away from Australia for nine years, most of them in the tropics. It was customary for missionaries to take a furlough every 5 years especially those working in tropical Africa with its dangers of malaria and sunstroke. I had been just one year at the School established to provide basic education for the children of Brethren missionaries, Sakeji in the Mwinilunga district of Northern Rhodesia.

It was time for even the most conscientious missionary to take a break. Especially a widow with four young children all of whom had suffered from malaria by then.

In her report letter of 20th June 1936, Mother mentions the decision to take a furlough at home. *"I would ask your special prayers as I and the children are booked to leave Cape Town for furlough on October 9th due in Melbourne November 2nd. Please pray that we may be used for His glory especially on the boat".*

This brave lady was going home without her husband. The journey from Livingstone to Cape Town via Johannesburg by rail and thence by sea to Melbourne, a protracted one in itself, was preceded by an epic four week voyage down the *Yambeji* as the river was known locally.

Mr. and Mrs. Logan accompanied us as far as Johannesburg.

It was 28th September 1937. The barge loaded with luggage and supplies under the arched canvas canopy, was beached on the white sand at the landing below the Chavuma falls. The waves lapped gently rocking the vessel that was to be our floating home for a month.

Sitting on the beach were the sixteen paddlers and captain, all of the Barotse tribe who knew the volatile river, its rapids and its seasonal moods almost instinctively and certainly better than the local Lwena or Lunda people. Their sixteen wood carved paddles lay in the barge eight to the fore and eight in the stern. Only the *kapitano* (captain) wore a shirt and shorts. The paddlers wore only a skirt of cloth or hide.

Raising her voice above the roar of the falls, Mother stood speaking to the one hundred or so people who had come to the river to bid us goodbye. The Logan children and the single missionaries were among the crowd. Farewell hymns were sung and the opportunity was not missed to speak one more word of the Gospel. Some shed tears, many wished us well. Would this astonishing white lady come back and continue her ministry, or was this really goodbye?

The family climbed into the barge taking a seat under the canopy of curved saplings stretched as an arch from the port to the lee side with a canvas tarpaulin stretched over it as protection from tropical sun and rain. *Kapitano Shilingi* commanded the paddlers to grasp the barge. Many of them waist deep and all with hands firmly on the vessel.

Shilingi's voice rang out: *"Futi madoda kuya."* Instantly the paddlers responded in unison to the refrain with one syllable: "cho!" as they shoved the vessel down from the beach and deeper into the water. Once more the cry: *"Futi madoda kuya ...."*

The words were not Lwena, but a dialect of Zulu and might be translated as: "Once again chaps, let's pull together". The song was often sung as a means of coordinating the timing of joint effort when heavy physical work was required.

To a man the paddlers responded to the cry, shouting: "cho", as they gave a last shove, springing into the barge and grabbing their paddles in one motion. A few swift strokes in unison and the barge was heading out to the deep water.

As it turned into the main current we looked ahead where a perfect rainbow spanned the river. The effect was remarkable in that there were no faint sections, the bright colours held their bold fullness across the entire bow, forming a perfect arch from bank to bank.

Perhaps this biblical symbol of promise given to Noah at the time of the flood was an appropriate promise to a more modern saint who had suffered such loss on these waters and laboured so diligently in the region. Was this a promise of a safe voyage on the great river that so often symbolised the glorious river of Mother's life?

Sixteen paddlers standing face forward, blades dipping in perfect timing with powerful strokes thrusting the barge faster than the current; sounds and sights of wildest Africa; landing for a quick lunch and camping at night near the water's edge, these were to be our daily routine for a month.

As we waved goodbye the barge moved away from the shore and the current began moving it swiftly down the mighty Zambezi. A last look upstream at the falls, its torrent belching through the gap in an awesome water spout, subliminally brought to the memory of an eight year old, the tragic event at that very place in May 1933.

The scenery along the river even to our accustomed eyes, was startlingly verdant at times, changing to white sand on which crocodiles lay basking in the sun and exotic bird life strutted or took off in flight displaying the brilliance of their plumage.

Especially during the dry season, but even now, herds of elephants were drawn to the water's edge and the banks were home to many migratory and wading birds. It was an adventure in a theatre of undisturbed natural beauty.

As old rivers tend to do, the Zambezi twisted and turned with each corner revealing a new and exciting vista. Tropical forest, steep cliffs with vegetation clinging to the rock formation, falling sheer into the swirling waters came to view. Then suddenly a shimmering stretch of white sand, the only footprints being those of a myriad of birds, antelope, lions, leopards and hippopotamus.

Invariably on the sand a crocodile or two lay basking in the sun. Temptingly open, the fierce jaws invited the winged living tooth-brush to clean off the carrion remaining from feeding on an unwary animal that had ventured too close to the water's edge.

At times, swinging around a corner would reveal ominous rocks rotruding in rapids of sparkling, fast flowing water.

Navigating a barge through rapids required considerable skill and knowledge of the probable depth at a particular time of the year. An alert and experienced kapitano standing on a cross bar to give him a better view, as well as prompt and powerful paddle strokes by sixteen paddlers in disciplined response to his one-syllabled and gestured commands, were essential to safety in a crocodile infested river, where the ability to swim was not necessarily adequate protection.

Around another corner the attractive scene of soft white beach sand would come into view. Myriads of birds from flamingos to the fish eagle, cormorants to kingfishers, would take flight leaving the sand covered by a million footprints. A crocodile or two basking lazily would shuffle off into the water or a herd of hippos splash snorting into the river.

Unable to resist the beauty of the inviting scene, where quite probably, no human had walked for a year or more, we would persuade Mother to have the barge beached, letting us run excitedly across the bleached soft stretch of sand just inches above the water level rippling at the edge.

One of the attractions of romping on these beaches was the phenomenon of the squealing sand. As each bare foot stabbed the powdery white sand, the beach emitted a loud squeal with an oich! oich! sound.

It was 68 years later before I met someone who had heard this sound and believed the story. Illona Povey now living in Durban, South Africa had lived along the Zambezi in the same area and was familiar with this fascinating experience.

Instead of beach, some of the river's banks were sheer cliffs dropping vertically into the water. The cliffs, had been formed by erosion often with a large section of earth and sand falling into the river and leaving an exposed face of firm sand, into which many swallows and other birds had burrowed making caves for nesting, safely out of reach of predators.

Lunch time involved looking for a suitable landing, a quick camp fire for tea and a snack, sitting on portable chairs at a folding table. My brother and I would amuse ourselves counting how many crocodiles could be seen coming to the surface. I remember one count of thirty sightings during the 30 minutes lunch time.

Sometimes we would do some line fishing with a bamboo stick for rod, a piece of twine, a piece of gourd for a float and a bent pin for a hook. In the clear Zambezi water visibility of the sandy or river weed bottom was often excellent. One could usually see fish swimming around the bait.

Not having a long line we were usually confined to smaller fish inshore. The river teemed with bream and tiger fish so occasionally a larger fish would have a go at the bait. My brother once lifted a sizeable bream out of the water before its weight, not far off his own, straightened the pin, letting the catch slide back into safety.

Just before sunset the tent, camp beds, canvas bath, hurricane lamps and other equipment would be carried on shore. A roaring camp fire near the tent and another for the paddlers would not only permit cooking of food but also deter at least some of Africa's wild life particularly hyenas, elephants or the big cats from venturing too close for comfort.

After the evening meal Mother would bring out her guitar, ask the sixteen Barotse paddlers, *Shillingi* the Barotse *kapitano* and a cook-boy, to gather around the camp fire where, led by this intrepid widow evangelist, we would sing gospel hymns in Lwena and hear once again the story of the redemptive work of *Kulixitu* (Christ) the Son of *Kalunga* (God).

Three days down river from Chavuma we arrived at Balovale, our nearest outpost of British civilisation.

Balovale was an interesting place for M.K.'s to stop over on a 4 week barge trip southwards.

The building quality of most of the government offices and houses of the officials was a cut above missionary homes. Brick walls and the existence of ceilings comprised the main difference. One of the features intriguing to M.K.'s was the smooth highly polished maroon floors.

The post office with its smell of ink, its polished counter and the bank of pigeon holes for mail sorting, was a world of its own. The inhabitants of this world were educated native clerks in glistening white suits wearing terribly important expressions wholly appropriate to their vastly elevated status.

Bertram P. Rudge, a brother in law of Gavin Mowat, owned a trading store at Balovale, besides running a mission. The Rudges were, so called, independent missionaries who were not only very hospitable to all who passed through Balovale but generously gave parcels of groceries and other supplies to fellow missionaries from time to time.

A reasonably regular barge service to and from Livingstone was operated and Rudge had a barge building and maintenance operation.

Barges, used for cargo and passenger transport, were well made of hand-planed boards fixed by screws to cross ribs and sealed with pitch. The water made the solid timber swell, thus making it leak-proof. The barge had no rudder, steering being achieved by the left and right paddlers at the stern. A rope of woven tree bark kept damp and curled up in the prow, provided a means of hauling the barge when required.

There being no roads accessible to motor transport until some years later, bees wax was exported down stream and all equipment and supplies not available in the district were shipped upstream.

George Anderson, a young Scottish missionary, who worked tirelessly as a missionary at Balovale, also made time to work in barge making. Anderson was an interesting man who could enthral a couple of M.K.'s for hours with Bible and other stories. Years later he became a sought-after preacher among the Brethren assemblies in South Africa. His style was exegetical with logical and easily followed structure. He would pause now and again to digress on a parenthetical, yet important issue, saying in his unmistakable Scottish accent, "What we want to notice in passing......".

Any single one of these parenthetical pauses usually contained material enough for a whole sermon on its own. The logical, yet poetic way, in which George Anderson interpreted and analysed the scriptures, seemed almost inspired at times, even to a sceptical M.K.

Soon we were off again heading downstream past the confluence of the Kabompo river to Chitokoloki, yet another Brethren mission station.

Chitokoloki was the work base of a very musical missionary couple Jim and Nora Caldwell. Jim had a baritone voice that could open the hardest heart to the gospel. His contribution to the music of the church including new compositions was unmatched. His native name was *Sakwimba,* Father of Song.

One of the airs doing the rounds among Western influenced natives at the time, was a melody which I always thought was a composition by Caldwell and which for the most part sounds uncommonly similar to the tune of "Under the Spreading Chestnut Tree". Strangely the same melody became popular in other parts of Africa with time, and amazingly surfaced as the tune for a political song about Africa. In its form "Nkosi Sikele iAfrika" it was in 1994 adopted as the official anthem of South Africa. If my understanding of the facts is correct, then the Soweto man buried in Braamfontein cemetery, Johannesburg and lauded as the composer, has probably had to explain to his maker just how he got the credit for the composition.

Nora Caldwell was sister to another missionary at Chitokoloki, Mrs George Suckling. Gordon, the Suckling M.K., was several years older than Walter and I, and became a very handsome young man, probably the most eligible bachelor between the Belgian Congo and Southern Rhodesia. Of course there were not many white bachelors in that region with whom to compete, but Gordon did make the perfect knight to carry off Peggy - one of the lovely sisters in the Fisher family about whom there is more in the chapter on Sakeji School.

Chitokoloki was also the home of Jean Caldwell, Jim *(Sakwimba)* and Nora's daughter, who a few years later would be eyed by my more handsome brother Walter. Jean later married one of our contemporaries at Sakeji School, Brian Fisher who held the record for sjambokking at the hands of Charles Nightingale the headmaster. (I was a good runner up in the thrashing stakes.)

Leaving Chitokoloki, the river widened further with the flow from the tributary Lunguebungu sourced in Angola and flowing past another Brethren mission station we knew as Lungevungu, where Mr and Mrs Hansen worked in solitary dedication.

The river meandered on past missions where so many of Mother's colleagues were stationed. The water course seemed occasionally to pause, as if focussing on memories of the scenery already traversed, only to reveal another distracting panorama of beauty around the next river bend. If the scenic variability reflected Mother's experience on the glorious river of her life, then perhaps the relentless flow symbolised her unwavering commitment.

We were now traversing a very lonely stretch during which we would not see another human being for 13 days. Night after night we disembarked before sunset. Routinely the paddlers and helpers cleared bush for camp, erected the tent, lit the camp fire and prepared for nightfall.

Walter and I would drop a line hoping for a catch. Then came the evening meal, the gospel meeting with Mother's faultless soprano voice ringing out across the waters, the guitar strumming in harmony and the paddlers singing in enjoyment.

Sleeping in a canvas tent that did not zip up, often meant sharing the comfort with natural creatures like chameleons, snakes and other curious or hungry undesirables.

Yet the tent with its unusual smell afforded a feeling of relative security, so that when the tropical rain deluged down upon it, one gave a little shiver of excitement and felt snug if not completely safe.

The routine at sunrise was a quick wash using the canvas basin, a breakfast of porridge and tea then packing up, lowering and rolling up the tent. Sometimes Walter and I used to enjoy standing inside the tent while the paddlers were lowering it and then crawling out of the folding canvas.

Soon the barge would be reloaded and we would embark to enjoy another day on the beautiful and wild waterway.

In some parts of the river we would encounter vast areas of beautiful water lilies, their scent and pastel colours beckoning us to pause on the journey and to watch water fowl walking on the flat leaves and pecking at insects and larvae.

Some several day's journey north of Barotseland, the *kapitano* announced we would have to disembark on reaching a series of rapids which could not be traversed by navigating around the rocks in the usual way. The flow was too fast and the rocks too treacherous for that. The method used here was to leave only two paddlers in the front of the barge while the remaining fourteen, standing on the river bank, would grasp a rope fastened to the rear of the barge.

The vessel thus lightened and not so deep in the water with most of the manpower holding rope, the *kapitano* would take up a position where he could observe both the threatening rocks and the jostled barge. He would give the command to gently let the rope out, as the two paddlers would steer around the vicious rocks until the barge was past the rushing white-waters and in the relative safety of the calmer and deeper river.

The rope was woven of bark strips from suitable trees and was amazingly strong provided it was kept moist. This was not difficult to achieve in a barge where a hand scooping up water from the river was all that was needed and where dipping into the river a day before use, could generally regenerate any loss of strength caused by drying out in the hot tropical sun.

At Balovale we had been joined by another barge carrying a cargo of bees-wax to Livingstone. The barge was manned by a team of the Lunda tribe. The Lunda did not have a reputation for river skills as had the Barotse whose habitat for much of the year was flooded. Rudge had arranged for his cargo vessel to accompany ours so that the paddlers and their Lunda captain might benefit from the guidance and example of our Barotse team.

Despite advice from the Barotse team, the Lundas had neglected their rope, which had become dry and brittle. Tribal animosity often characterised relationships in Africa and still does. One of the symptoms of such animosity is that advice from another tribe is treated with disdain or casual bravado.

As the rope holding the Lunda barge, was being let out, the two paddlers were making heavy weather of the steering job. The barge being heavily laden with its cargo of wax and low in the water, began swinging precariously from side to side, skirting the jagged rocks with only inches to spare.

The rope team struggled a little but were taking the strain, leaning backward as they slowly fed the rope out.

Suddenly the rope unravelled and parted. The entire anchoring team fell backwards to the ground and the barge carrying its cargo and two frightened paddlers, was swept down stream. Ahead, another threatening series of brown, jagged rocks jutted out from the white foaming current and who knew how many rugged boulders lurked just beneath the surface.

The paddlers picked themselves up and responded to the shouted command from the Barotse *kapitano* to dive into the river and try to hold the barge. Some clambered into it to assist the two paddlers steering. Thus did the scorned Barotse captain, despite having to observe from a difficult vantage point below the cataract, save the barge and its cargo.

A few days later we reached the confluence of two major rivers the Lwena (one of two tributaries with the same name) and the Luanginga. Joining the Zambezi at almost the same point, they turned it into a vast flowing sea.

As the terrain flattens, the vast flow, swollen by early tropical summer rains, annually floods the plains so that in some areas the horizon in every direction is shimmering Zambezi water. A barge heading southwards in this inland sea with the current no longer a guide to the right direction and with no navigating equipment, requires a *kapitano* with directional skills besides those he needs to apply at cataracts and rapids.

Having regained confidence by now and with no rapids to intimidate, the Lunda team pushed ahead one day, disappearing

over the watery horizon. They had paddled several miles up what turned out to be the tributary Lwena before realising that our Barotse powered barge was out of sight.

There were no landmarks to guide on that vast stretch of inland sea. Even what looked like islands were often large floating clumps of turf broken away from the shore upstream. Even possession of a compass would have been useless to them. The sun position provided some indication of direction. Only the knowledge and patience of the Barotse captain enable us to locate and link up with the cargo vessel and its anxious manpower before nightfall.

We were now entering Barotseland the home of this river-trained tribe referred to by some as MaLozi. Wallace Logan enjoyed telling us about the interesting practices and culture of the area affected so dramatically by the seasonal flooding of the plains.

When the first summer rains bring relief to the thirsty plains of Africa, myriads of migrating wildebeest and zebra gather on Liuwa Plain.

The famous king Lewanika of the Barotses who enjoyed the ear of Queen Victoria during the latter part of the nineteenth century when boundaries were being drawn, managed to secure promises of a measure of special treatment, if not actual independence, from the rest of Northern Rhodesia. This was to cause problems for the Zambian government later when Uhuru came and federation was being mooted.

One of Lewanika's claims to fame was his annual ceremonial move to higher ground when the floods came down, turning the farmlands of the MaLozi into a mighty lake so that the people must move to higher ground.

Logan had a special interest in this annual event and had earlier filmed the ceremony.

It is known as the Kuomboka, literally "to get out of water", and this annual exodus, now conducted by his heirs in late February, takes the form of a ceremonial procession of small boats and dugout canoes led by the massive royal barge.

The paddlers were dressed in royal ceremonial style wearing skins and headdress decorated with feathers which swayed in unison at each stroke of the paddle. Only the most skilled and talented paddlers participated in the summer move from the mainstream river and back again when the dry winter season came.

In his "Kuomboka : Ancient Wisdom of the Malozi", Andrew Rooke vividly describes the ceremony:

"The paramount chief's barge bears the legendary name of Nalikwanda and it is truly a craft of royal proportions with room for the Chief, his attendants, the royal musicians, and at least one hundred traditionally-clad paddlers. It is an impressive sight to see this great craft gliding deftly along the murky Zambezi waters with the huge maoma drums booming over the staccato rhythm of the Lozi salimbas (xylophones) calling the people to follow to the safety of the high ground".

The *Kuomboko* is still practised by his descendants including Yeta II who was the reigning chief at the time of our passage through Barotseland.

When we arrived, a few small islands dotted the inland sea. We saw local fishermen canoeing between the tall stalks of maize and spearing fish where weeks before they had harvested their crop.

The dry land was several kilometres away from the regular winter mainstream. Nearby Mongu-Lealui a small town, was built on slightly higher ground. Its trading stores, post office, government offices and road access attracted the natives who would get there by canoe in summer but had to walk the distance in winter.

Chief Yeta II showed some initiative in obtaining colonial government assistance for diverting some of the Zambezi water into a canal which flowed very close to Mongu and then flowed onwards and back into the mainstream. This permitted canoes and barges even in the dry season, to come within a short climb up the bluff on which stood Mongu.

As the seasonal flood was not yet at its height our barge made use of the canal enabling us to visit Mongu where Mother and the Logans greeted and visited government officials.

As at Balovale, the M.K.'s were struck by the standard icons of a colonial African outpost, the polished floors of the District Commissioner's office and his home, the brilliant poinsettia in the gardens and the red fez with black tassel worn by bustling, ubiquitous 'messengers'.

Trading stores were surrounded by scores of villagers many of whom had no money and seemed happy to gather slouching or leaning against a pole on the shady verandas savouring the latest gossip or mesmerised by the evidence of the white trader's commercial acumen and his selection of cloth, salt, knives and other merchandise in demand. The inevitable hand or foot operated sewing machine buzzed away industriously.

Back on the inland sea again finding a camping site for the night presented a problem. Not only are islands few and far between at flood season, but every possible living creature from rats to army ants and some carnivores are often marooned on such islands, making them inhospitable as camping sites. What is worse, the
floods often erode away large chunks of turf from the river bank which float down into the flooded plains and which, to the uninitiated eye, can be mistaken for stable islands on which to camp. Often the soil has washed off leaving only a clump of the vegetation floating.

Fortunately the Barotse *kapitano,* Shillingi, now in home territory, knew where to locate winter's highest hills now providing refuge as islands. We camped on several such islands, as we paddled through Barotseland. Once after dark, the roar of hungry lions echoed across the water from a nearby island and we were glad to have selected what we thought was a hazard free island to camp on.

Deep into the night we were awakened with our bodies covered by stinging red army ants. These were the pests that had devoured our canaries leaving their clean white bones lying on the cage floor - the dreaded *Eciton burchelli.* The bites were painful and frightening as these red warriors attacked even our eyes.

My twin sisters were crying. Quickly Mother lit the paraffin hurricane lamps and called to the crew. We brushed off the voracious insects as best we could and got back on to the beached barge where we waited for the sunrise, the water lapping gently against the boards and in the early light, huge eddies of the rising flood rippling past us to the chirping of crickets and water fowl.

Our voyage had brought us to a point 300 kilometres upstream from the Victoria falls. This was Ngonye falls, where the Zambezi tumbles over a broad expanse of eight cascades across the 1.5 kilometres river width, near Sioma.

The land fault causing this magnificent spectacle makes the river un-navigable. On arrival at Sioma therefore, we had to disembark and the paddlers packed all our supplies and belongings onto an ox wagon. A team of oxen supplied by the local trader was yoked in and we clambered on top of the luggage facing a tiring day in the burning sun as we lurched and jostled our way towards the re-launching spot below the falls. The empty barge was towed over the hot sand by another team of oxen.

It was a relief to reload and launch the barge at the narrow strip of beach surrounded by towering cliffs of dark basalt rock. After a welcome night's rest, camped on the shore beside the vessel, we re-embarked and proceeded down the unique waterway.

A few days downstream, the crew suddenly dropped their paddles to the floor of the barge, sat themselves on the side timbers and clapped their hands in unison, uttering no word. The unattended barge drifted with the current. This was no strike. Strikes were to come much later when work began to be viewed not as a benefit and privilege but as an imperial conspiracy.

After six minutes the crew resumed their positions dipping their paddles and thrusting the barge forward as before. Mother asked the captain the reason for this ritual. *Shilingi* told us that many decades before, a great chief, and ancestor of Yeta and Lewanika, had together with his entire capital village disappeared into a massive yawning crevice that opened up in the earth with a terrifying roar and flying boulders, falling trees and blinding dust.

Having swallowed man, woman, child, dog, sheep, goat and chicken, the fissure closed as quickly as it had opened. The pause in the paddling had been a mark of respect for the victims and to placate the great spirits responsible for the sudden tragedy.

A few days downstream we beached the barge near a large native village. Drawn up on the shore next to ours, was an empty barge with a large hole at the rear end, the result of an attack by a hippopotamus.

As we stood on the shore before finding a spot on which to camp, a crowd of curious natives gathered around staring at the rare sight of a white missionary lady and her young family and wondering at the interesting camping equipment they had brought with them.

The usual scrawny village dog was enjoying the excitement, sniffing around at the water's edge when suddenly there was turbulence in the water and with a tremendous splashing the dog disappeared yelping beneath the surface, firmly held in the relentless jaws of a crocodile. In another second the waters were calmly lapping the shore line as if the event had been an illusion.

Sesheki on the left bank was an interesting place to stop partly because it was believed that Dr. David Livingtone sat in the shade of a magnificent tree which still stood at the time of our visit.

Logan who with his wife had shared the journey with us, posed for his photograph under the tree, jokingly wondering whether that would make the tree even more famous.

Having seen no river traffic up to this point on the journey, we now noticed an occasional barge marked 'Wenela', transporting recruited natives to work on the mines in South Africa.

Just a few days from the end of our river journey we passed an invisible point in the centre of river where the boundaries of four countries meet, reputedly the only such place in the world. The countries were then named Northern and Southern Rhodesia, South West Africa and Bechuanaland.

The spot is at Katima Mulilo on the eastern point of the Caprivi Strip which today is a part of Namibia, at the time South West Africa, a former German colony.

Barges could not proceed beyond a certain point above the Victoria Falls, so when after four weeks, we reached Catambora, our scenic journey down the great Yambezi came to an end. Transport into Livingstone was by ox wagon.

With some sadness yet gratitude we bade farewell to the captain and crew who, having been paid their wages, were left sufficient rations to serve them for the return journey upstream.

And so atop a creaking ox wagon, this group of travel weary explorers emerged from the wilderness staring in wonder at the unfamiliar sights of tarred streets, telegraph poles, strange buildings and so many shops and motor vehicles. Dorothy and Margaret had never been in a town and Walter and I had been babies when we left Roodepoort.

Our train to Cape Town via Johannesburg was due to leave in a day or two so we were kindly accommodated at the missionary home run by the Paris Mission. It was there we tasted out first ice cream. When my sister Dorothy took her first lick she exclaimed "It's hot!"

The opportunity to see the grandeur of the Victoria Falls was not missed. Watching the cascade of water made me think of the many miles it had travelled through dark forests, sunny plains, collecting more water from so many tributaries. One thought of it as the birth place of so many fish, exotic and tasty, and its role in quenching the thirst of so much dry and dusty land and of the many beautiful animals, before finally taking this majestic leap.

I thought of the large languid inland sea in Barotseland and the many cataracts and rapids over which that water had tumbled and was now roaring over the greatest of all cataracts on its ineffable and mysterious way down to the Indian Ocean.

During the hot and sooty steam train journey through Southern Rhodesia to Johannesburg we managed to persuade Mother to buy us the shell of a tortoise that was offered at one of the lonely stations. It would add to the curios Mother was taking to excite the supporters in Melbourne. To our astonishment as the train slowly gained speed leaving the station behind, four reptilian legs and a frightened head emerged from the shell and, like it or not, we had a pet to look after.

Mother was not sure whether live animals could be legally imported into the Union of South Africa, so she told me not to talk about our new pet and to pass on the message to Walter. As the train puffed slowly into Mafeking station, the brakes screeching and the bustling platform coming to view, we each looked out of a window to see what other marvels of civilised Africa were available. Mother heard me shouting to Walter with my neck well out of the window, "Mother says we mustn't talk about the tortoise". Walter replied equally loudly, "Why what's wrong with the tortoise?" I felt myself jerked back vigorously into the train by a maternal hand.

Fortunately we stayed a few days in Johannesburg with Mr and Mrs Coleridge, who had years before been so helpful to my father in the printing work. They had a couple of tortoises in their yard and offered to take our pet over if we allowed them to name him Chavuma.

The missionary connection proved helpful again as we spent a few days with retired missionaries Mr and Mrs Pugsley in the Kensington suburb of Johannesburg. Their home, always open to travelling missionaries was situated against one of the rocky ridges for which the Witwatersrand is so well-known, and just below a monument which many readers will recognise as having been erected to honour members of the Transvaal Scottish regiment who fell during the Anglo Boer war.

Here Mother and her family bade farewell to Wallace and Ruth Logan and continued on to Cape Town by rail, spending a few days at the Wellwood Missionary home in Fishhoek. Wellwood was another Brethren facility so useful to missionaries en route to or from the African field.

Embarking on an ocean-going 'barge' the S.S. Themistocles, on October 9th 1936, was just another of the many new and strange experiences for these Children of Chavuma as we shared in Mother's well deserved furlough.

Mother on Board S.S. Themistocles 1937

11. Melbourne Intermission

No luxury liner this. Yet to us it seemed like a floating palace with its comfortable cabin bunks, lounges, swimming pool and even a barber's shop. On the whole a very civilised way of travelling. It certainly had the edge on tramping through rain forests or hot plains, despite the old steamer being on its last journey prior to scrapping.

One of the lounges had a piano. I recall listening to a passenger playing Chopin's "Fantaisie Impromptu in C# Minor". Mother, who enjoyed the music, told us that it had been the melody of this composition to which the words of the popular song, "I'm always chasing rainbows" had been written. The skill with which the pianist's fingers executed the beautiful and complicated sequences fascinated me.

Equally memorable was the group of four passengers who made attractive harmony with a banjo, a guitar and two harmonicas. One of the pieces they played was the Maori melody, popular at the time as "Now is the Hour".

Deck quoits, shuffle-paddle and swimming made the journey enjoyable to the five from the jungle. That is, of course, after we had become accustomed to the roll of the vessel.

Sailing eastwards around the Cape, noted for its rough seas, we were sitting on deck one afternoon, when Walter, offering to go down to the cabin, asked Mother, "shall I bring up the biscuit tin". Mother's sense of humour surfaced even at the most uncomfortable moment, as she replied: "Bring up anything you like - I could!". Someone who heard this example of Mother's spontaneous wit, described her as a frivolous missionary, a remark which was later relayed back to her.

For the inevitable fancy dress party, Mother prepared two matching florally decorated dresses out of bright coloured crepe paper for the twins. For Walter, she borrowed a girl's wig and dressed him in drag (though it wasn't called that of course). For me she used an old sack, cut four holes for legs in the corners, laced up the open end around my neck, put a workman's cap on my head, a sliver of black boot polish on my cheek and pinned a card on the sack stating: "Got the sack!"

The twins and I were home and dry with a prize each, when somebody shouted to the judges that Walter was actually a boy. He got a prize too and some hearty wolf whistles.

We arrived in Melbourne harbour on November 2nd 1936. While packing and dressing in the cabin, with excitement we watched, through the porthole, a small steamer come out to deliver the pilot. A few moments later there was a knock on the cabin door. It was Walter Sandbach our uncle. What an emotional moment as he embraced his widowed sister back from the dark continent. He had made special arrangements to be ferried out to our ship with the pilot.

For some months we stayed in East Malvern with uncle Walter, his wife Dorothy and our cousins Eddie and Allison. On seeing us, Eddie and Allison expressed surprise that, despite being born in Africa, we were not black.

The experience of settling into an Australian school, living in a well run and well equipped home and learning many new games, tricks and customs from our cousins, was novel and exciting.

Just going for a walk in a park with its manicured lawns and perfectly tended flower beds, taken to a kiosk by Eddie and introduced to liquorice using actual money to pay for it, were all part of assimilating a different life style from what we had known.

To us Eddie was something of a whiz-kid making sparks from electricity which he generated by turning a handle and revealing many other mysteries of science to us. Allison was the kind and loving cousin who showed us the way to school, helped us avoid the bullies and warned us about the crotchety lady whose house we had to pass on the way and who would soak you with her garden hose if you lingered.

Meeting our maternal Granddad Edward Sandbach, son of the gold pioneer and our uncle Keith as well as 'aunties' Louie and Dora, added to the feeling that this was a different world previously only imagined from Mother's descriptions.

At 56 Crown Street, Flemington, Granddad Sandbach and Keith regaled us with their music on banjo, harmonica, piano and drinking glasses filled with water to varying levels to produce the required scale of notes, when struck with a spoon.

Paternal grandmother Mary Anne Barnett, a widow, lived with her son, our uncle Alfred at 68 Argyll St, Moonie Ponds. When Grandmother passed away shortly after our arrival in Melbourne, uncle Alf Barnett kindly suggested that we move to 68 Argyll Street where Mother was able to keep house and where we, settled in to the Moonie Ponds school.

Uncle Alf was studying theology at university, later becoming Presbyterian Moderator for Tasmania. The house where Fred Barnett had grown up barely survived the onslaught of the country bumpkins from Africa. Blocking the water borne sewage system (a novel device to us) and damaging Uncle Alf's favourite shrub, were just a few of the uncivilised things we white Africans managed to perpetrate.

Alf's patience was sorely tried when, chasing Walter down the passage one day, he ducked out of my way and I rushed on pushing my arm through the stained glass pane of the back door, sustaining not even a scratch by way of punishment. Alf had the window repaired with a plain piece of plywood which stared out at me in rebuke every time I passed.

Our fellow pupils found our accent amusing and gave us some teasing. The teachers were quick to recognise our African origin as valuable, and we were often sent to other classes to tell them about our experiences and to answer questions. I recall particular interest in our many servants and their names like Kakweji (the moon), Moni, Hoxi and others. We were treated with awe more appropriate to travellers from outer space and soon became adept at introducing touches of melodrama into the stories for effect.

Mother gave considerable time to speaking at meetings particularly about the mission work. She had packed and shipped a large solid wooden case containing curios including the skin of a python killed near our house, some idols and African artefacts. These made excellent props for the meetings, stirring considerable interest. Clearly the Australian customs department were then more relaxed than they are today.

On Sundays we would hasten up Puckle street to catch the tram to Brunswick where the Brethren assembly was located. For the first time, we M.K.'s were able to see the format and model of services which the missionaries had been endeavouring to reproduce in the African context of illiteracy and primitive culture.

Afterwards we would often be invited for lunch to the home of one of the members. The opulence we encountered for the first time in some homes was an indicator of the potential lifestyle our parents had given up to answer the missionary call.

Melbourne shop windows at Christmas time were breathtaking. I recall the Coles toy window with an animated tropical scene in which a monkey pushed and pulled a Christmas cracker in and out of a crocodile's jaws cleverly avoiding the closing snap each time. A touch of Zambezi in a Melbourne departmental emporium! Mother could hardly draw us away from the displays.

City life revealed many sights which surprised us. Looking up at the tall high-rise buildings blocking out the sky except for a narrow strip above the street, my eye caught an extraordinary sight on the ninth floor of a skyscraper. The wall facing the street was glazed to the floor, revealing a host of beautifully dressed couples whirling gracefully and swiftly, their footwork so nimble as, in unison, their bodies swayed and turned in time to the rhythm of the music.

When Mother called it dancing, I found it difficult to equate this artistically eye-catching performance with what we had known as dancing in African villages. The only common factor was rhythm. The artistry, the music, the dress and the clean environment, seemed worlds apart.

Melbourne was hit by an epidemic of poliomyelitis which closed many schools. With commendable speed the authorities launched an inoculation programme and supplied printed material to every home enabling, at least, some basic education to continue. Mother's natural gift for teaching enabled her to provide support and motivation so that we derived maximum benefit from the material. The epidemic subsided in a matter of months.

We saw our first snow on the slopes of Mount Donnabuang where we picnicked with the Sandbach's. Eddie took with him a kitchen tray which afforded us some fun tobogganing on the strange frozen white powder.

Visiting Mother's aunt Dora Cole (nee Sandbach) who had a house in the country near Melbourne, we saw something of Australian sheep farming on the nearby farm owned by Dora's son Alf. We may have been country bumpkins but milking cows stabling horses and playing on a haystack, were new to us. Barbed wire was another unfamiliar feature.

One evening Walter and I were chasing each other on the farm in the dusk. Running from me he ducked underneath a tightly stretched single strand of barbed wire and, not seeing it, I received deep scratches on chin and cheek which required stitches and left me with a souvenir of lasting minor scars.

Mother and Family: Melbourne 1937

Uncle Alf, who was always whistling or humming a happy tune (his favourite being "Poor Little Angeline") seemed close to the land and at ease with the world. He had one enemy. That was the ubiquitous and hungry rabbit. He hired a trapper who was paid on a per-bunny basis and did well out of the skins. The meat sold well too.

Mother recorded a number of gospel songs in a Melbourne recording studio. Neither the old fashioned 78 rpm records nor the limitations of technology of the thirties were able to disguise the quality and timbre of her lovely voice. Walter still has one of the old records to this day.

Another memory was made in a photographic studio where the picture on these pages was taken. The classically refined look of the dressed up Barnett M.K.'s posing around their adored mother, says something for the civilising effect of 11 months in the land of kangaroos and billabongs.

Scarcely a year had passed and Mother was ready to return to her work. Many advised against this but her determination was unwavering. We returned on the same S.S. Themistocles which seemed to have survived its forecast execution and were assured that this was indeed its last voyage.

In a letter dated 1st April 1938 published by Australian Missionary Tidings, Mother writes of the "short furlough" and the journey back. She records being met at the Durban docks by a kind businessman Archie Louden.

We stayed over at the Concorde missionary home with its boarding school atmosphere and uninspired fare. The inevitable spinster in charge seemed to exude vibrations of discipline and I recall some poor missionary guest getting into serious trouble over putting his serviette into the wrong coloured ring provided.

Mother writes of enjoying our short stay in Bulawayo, Southern Rhodesia with Mrs. Sims, wife of Chavuma co-founder Bert and mother of John, who later married dear Eleanor Logan.
Her letter goes on to record a three week wait at Livingstone resulting from damage caused to the barge as it traversed one of the rapids, coming from Chavuma to fetch us. It had to be repaired at Sioma.

For part of that waiting period we stayed in some holiday huts at the edge of the mighty Zambezi close to the Victoria Falls and in sight of the "Smoke that Thunders". Fishing every day for nearly two weeks was the most pleasant wait Walter and I had ever had to put up with.

Mother too enjoyed the quiet and peaceful rest. While the furlough in Melbourne ought to have been a period of rest, she had, as recorded, been very busy in report back meetings, and housekeeping for four school going children and a brother-in-law.

Here camped at the edge of the river that typified her life in so many ways, she enjoyed being "beside the still waters" if only for a brief while.

The barge journey upstream, normally a six week trip took only four weeks since the paddlers were anxious to get home having already lost three weeks due to the damage.

This example of worker incentive, got us to Chitokoloki for Christmas dinner arriving back home at Chavuma on 30th Dec 1937.

Mother wrote:

"We praise the Lord for his great help as we passed through the rapids for none of the crew were hurt in any way or caught by the crocs. There were many on the bank in the river. We saw some everyday. On our arrival here we received a royal welcome and crowds came to greet us. The Christians sang continuously as we wended our way up the hill. We rejoice in being back again with the people we love."

Scarcely able to rest after the long journey from Melbourne, Mother wrote: *"After a week here it was necessary for me to take a hurried trek with the Logan children and my two boys to meet Albert Horton near Cazombo, who took the children on to Sakeji in his truck."*

Sakeji School

12. Sakeji School

It is not difficult to understand the significant role Sakeji school played in the life of an M.K.

The school was founded in 1925 specifically to provide primary education to the children of Brethren missionaries. Apart from a few mission schools on stations run often by dedicated amateurs and limited to lower grades, there was no suitable establishment anywhere in that region. Without Sakeji, M.K.'s would have had to be separated from their parents for schooling and sent 'home' to the British Isles, USA, Australia, Canada or New Zealand. In a very real sense Sakeji School kept missionaries on the field.

The school's internet website http://sakeji.marcato.org, in April 2003, provides the following description:

"Sakeji School is a Christian primary boarding school situated near Ikelenge in a small finger of land which lies between Angola and Congo, in the remote northern tip of the North Western Province of Zambia. It is 70 kilometres north of Mwinilunga and 600 kilometres (about eight hours drive) from Kitwe.

The school takes its name from the Sakeji River, a tributary of the Zambezi River which is itself not far from the school on the Zambia-Congo watershed at an altitude of approximately 1400 m. At this altitude the climate is pleasant, with warm days and cool evening temperatures, especially during the dry season months in June and July. The average annual rainfall is 1400mm, almost all of which falls between October and April.

The school site is very attractive, and overlooks the Sakeji River, which provides both hydro-electric power for the school and a pleasant recreational environment for the children. Despite its remote location Sakeji is able to provide excellent boarding amenities and modern educational facilities.

Sakeji can accommodate up to one hundred students, but presently there are fifty four, representing some ten different nationalities. Almost all of these are boarders between the ages of 6 and 13. The staff usually includes 14 missionary teachers and care-givers from Europe, North America and Australasia, who minister to the educational, spiritual, physical and emotional needs of the children. Other support staff are employed locally by the school to assist with maintenance, catering, laundry and other domestic duties.

The school is supplied with fresh meat and dairy products by Hillwood Farms, while fresh fruit and vegetables are purchased regularly from local growers. Other foodstuffs and supplies, which are readily available in Zambia today, are brought by truck from the Copperbelt towns. By means of short wave radio, daily contact is maintained with other mission stations and with mission support personnel in the Copperbelt towns".

The web-site is worth a visit though the buildings and facilities are more vast and far more comfortable than at my time. We had no hydro-electric power or wave radio. A small wind-charger supplied limited power for charging batteries.

In the thirties, Hillwood farm across the river, owned by the ffolliat Fisher family, provided food for the school. On the farm was a native trading store and a Brethren assembly hall attended every Sunday by all at Sakeji.

Today this beautiful area through which the Sakeji river flows has become known for its unique species of avifauna and rain forest belt. It has thirty or more unique species and is the home of the Tree Pangola and the White-nosed monkey.

One of the beautiful wild flowers typical of the area is the flame lily *(gloriosa)* known by Sakeji pupils as "doctor's joy" even to this day. The flower was so named because of Dr. Walter Fisher's love for it and perpetuated because the resident physician at Kalene hospital, Dr Julyan Hoyt, so admired its beauty.

The Nchila Wildlife Reserve has recently been established by the grandson of ffoliat Fisher, Peter who now runs the Hillwood Farms.

The web-site of the Reserve provides the following description of the territory, where Sakeji School was established:

"Here, on Hillwood Farm, the Fisher family has grown coffee for several generations. Part of Hillwood has been set aside as a nature reserve and there is a wonderful mixed habitat of woodlands, grassland, and forest. Based in small chalets in the reserve itself, we will spend the days exploring the reserve and making day trips to several excellent birding areas nearby.

The Sakeji River

High on the list is the source of the Zambezi River, only a few hours drive from Hillwood, where a spring marks the start of this mighty river. As well as the excitement of being at this legendary spot, there is a strip of West African rainforest that covers the source and contains several very unusual birds. In fact, from a birding perspective, the area is one of the most productive in the whole of south-central Africa, as over 20 species on the Zambian list are found only here, and many of these are specialties of the forests of the Congo basin, an area currently fairly inaccessible to tourists".

Teachers at Sakeji were dedicated professionals who lived by the same "faith" principle as did other Brethren missionaries.

With forty pupils and only three classrooms, several grades shared rooms. We were distributed between three dormitories each in a separate building of mud and wattle walls and thatched roof with no ceiling. Sakeji had a tennis court and a large sports field.

There was a small airy building at one end of the playground where we would meet for chorus singing just before walking to the nearby kitchen and dining house for supper.

The headmaster, Charles Nightingale, a stern but competent man was a widower with four children. His wife, one of the Fisher clan, had died in childbirth leaving twin girls. His sister Edith was the caterer, taught music and looked after the twins.

Besides Lyndon Hess, the deputy head, there were two single teachers Hilda Harston and Hilda Kelly. Ruth Hess took turns at catering and also taught occasionally. These dedicated people also found time to conduct mission work among the native people.

Besides the normal educational subjects, scripture was an important major. This complemented the emphasis which the brethren placed on scripturally based doctrine. Our Bible history charts were works of art which helped us in mentally arranging Old Testament chronology.

The beautiful Sakeji river, a tributary of the Zambezi and too small at that point to be inhabited by crocodiles, provided us with a natural swimming area as well as fine beach sand amidst luscious river palms and other tropical flora. The river had been partially dammed and a diving board erected.

On our return from Melbourne in 1938, the Barnetts had, in 14 months, assimilated an Australian accent. Having been tormented by our fellow pupils at the Moonie Ponds School for a peculiar way of talking, and so, quickly adopted the local pronunciation, we now suffered a similar fate at Sakeji, where we were mocked with remarks such as: "Did you say *Oi arroived at Sakaiji to doie?*"

This was my second year at Sakeji. It had not been long into my first year before Miss Kelly realised that I was endemically an affront to all she held dear. Perhaps my rural Zambezi background jarred upon the sensitivities engendered by her much more civilised English origin.

At seven, without a father's guiding hand and having never been to school, there were doubtless some rough edges which presented a challenge or, perhaps even a gauntlet, to Hilda Kelly. My Australian ancestry did not help much I'm sure.

In addition to that, I was prone to deviate from rulings dictated by her especially when I perceived a more efficient shortcut. This she saw as laziness and wilful disdain for authority.

The normal appellation I received from her was "you chump".

Her solution was to pull me around by my ears, in order to humiliate me before the class, a practice reckoned by some to account for their size (my ears that is). At any rate the natives nicknamed me *kambondo,* the name of a particular kind of mukishi, a dervish with large ear lobes.

There can be no doubt that my frequent omission of full stops in prep-work was an intensely annoying habit and was rewarded with large red ink ones which she inserted. As soon as the page was full of these red signals I was granted a visit to the Head.

Nightingale was a very busy man and entitled to assume that, if Kelly an accredited Christian missionary teacher had sent me to him, then dispensing a thrashing with the hippo hide was naturally the appropriate response. Soon my own hide was tough too, and though at the age of seven, weeping normally came easily to me, I no longer cried when bending over for three of the best.

Anne Fisher of Hillwood Farm and granddaughter of the venerated Dr. Walter Fisher, was a really lovely girl who brightened my day by being seated next to me in the classroom. I learned from her brother Paul recently that Anne (now Wyatt) married a lucky Englishman in 1948. They are now doing mission work in Zambia.

Anne was artistic and recited poetry with a charming lisp which beguiled everyone including Miss Kelly. The fact that Anne was useless at mathematics and often craved my willing help, escaped Kelly completely. Most of the time Anne got good marks for cheating at mathematics. However when I got it wrong we both did. To Hilda Kelly, this was proof that I had cheated from Anne and alas, that meant another visit to Nightingale.

Even the children of missionaries required dentistry from time to time. The Brethren were fortunate in having Theo Deubler based at Chitokoloki mission and willing to travel as an itinerant dentist to other stations including Sakeji School.

His portable equipment would make a curious museum piece today. The drill was powered by pedalling. A large fly wheel drove a smaller pulley higher up the structure. The victim's school mates took turns at pedalling this apparatus which would have been at home in a torture chamber, while Deubler attended to the business end of the equipment. Every now and then the pedal-pushing school-mate would loose concentration, and revolutions would be lost with concomitant gain in pain for the patient. Deubler would remonstrate, whereupon the pedaller would instantly resume his pedalling pace before Deubler had time to re-focus, often resulting in the now speeding drill burrowing into the victim's gum or cheek.

My 'bucked' teeth, caused by the second row growing out before the first lot were ready to leave, were a challenge to any self- respecting dentist. Braces were either not invented or not easy to come by in the jungle. Deubler therefore gave me a 9cm metal rod with an ominously sharp curve at each end. This, I was supposed to use to lever the defective teeth into line. It was so painful and inconvenient that I lost the thing pretty soon.

At the next visit, about six months year later, instead of berating me, the kindly dentist conscientiously gave me another lever and gave Kelly another kind of mouthful for not supervising me. While I enjoyed her chagrin, I knew she relished having this new terror for me and I was thereafter hounded daily to use the weapon. Ingenuity enabled me to feign pain while exerting no pressure on the teeth. This excellent subterfuge saved me considerable discomfort and resulted in the teeth growing back into line of their own accord.

Perhaps it was a matter of mind over molars or just that I had inherited canny canines. Now, an octogenarian, and 'long in tooth', not one of my original teeth is missing and they all still point in the normal direction.

Teachers used to meet in the lounge of Charles Nightingale's home on Sunday evening for Bible reading and a 'sing-song' of hymns around the piano. We who were quartered in that building, and by then in bed with lights out, used to listen to the singing and enjoy the music especially when a really talented pianist happened to be visiting, such as Charlie Stokes.

Kelly's most demeaning punishment for me was to insist that on a Sunday evening, clad in my pyjamas, my colleagues all in bed, I bring her my rewritten school work into the lounge to be ticked off in front of the entire teaching staff who were enjoying their social evening, The hippo hide was better any day than that traumatic experience of shame.

In an unwittingly masterful act of motivation Kelly once prophesied that I would not manage to attain matriculation. This worked so well that I matriculated with honours and won the Dux scholar award at the Ermelo High School, South Africa.

No wonder years later I used to fantasize that one day I would own a red sports car and would drive into the Sakeji campus with a roaring exhaust and the squeal of brakes, stopping in a cloud of dust, which would envelope a spluttering Hilda Kelly in delicious revenge.

Interestingly, forty-seven years later I did acquire a red Nissan ZX280 sports model but, by then, dear Hilda had gone to meet her maker and no longer in a position to be much impressed by the more flamboyant evidence of my material success.

A few years later when Lyndon Hess succeeded as head, Miss Harston took over the onerous task of teaching me. To my amazement she actually discovered that I was very good at arithmetic, won many spelling B's and even had a sense of humour. This recognition developed my confidence enormously. The hippo hidings suddenly stopped and my fortunes generally improved.

The four Fisher girls were all talented artistically and were gifted poets. Mrs Fisher ran a competition at the school offering prizes for the best poem. It was a dead cert that her daughters would collect the first four prizes. The contest followed the Easter "objects" competition run by the school, in which we made presentations with a biblical theme on the sandy banks of the Sakeji river, using natural materials such as flowers, grasses, palm and other leaves, frangipani, bark, natural cork and other materials that lent themselves to artistic endeavour.

I had taken my presentation theme from New Testament parable of the barren fig tree which, as you will recall, was axed for being fruitless. I carved an axe from wood with a pen knife and used the main branch of a wild shrub for the fallen tree and its erect stump. The text was written, with river pebbles laid in sand. It received a commendation.

In keeping with my tendency towards short cuts, I decided to lean on an existing success as a theme for the poetry competition. My four verse poem was about the barren fig tree and the moral lesson to be drawn. The lyrics contained a repetitive chorus that was never going to remind anyone of Wordsworth or Thackeray and went something like this:

"So here's the lesson for us all

For the big and for the small"

Mrs Fisher and Miss Harston were the judges. The announcement of the winning entry shattered all expectations. First was Gavin Barnett, the Fisher girls taking the honours after me. Some of the Fishers were more dazed than amazed and said so. Not Anne though. She owed me too many correct Maths solutions to think I had nothing in my head.

I often wondered what Kelly would have said. Perhaps the ear- pulling had triggered off a latent capacity for the creative arts.

I suppose most of us have looked back in amusement at the events which helped to develop our confidence in a competitive world.

During the Second World War we used to gather round the single radio and listen to the BBC news so beautifully articulated by the reader in a low resonant voice.

On one occasion, having caught a severe throat cold my, as yet, unbroken voice was temporarily lowered to such an extent that I found I could imitate an adult male voice rather well. I found a cardboard tube to use as an amplifier, hid behind an open door between two classrooms and, in a deep resounding voice and my best imitation of British accent, announced: "This is the British Broadcasting Corporation. Here is the news".

In two minutes I had a crowd of fellow pupils pushing into the classroom to find out who the visitor was. When I emerged from behind the door, I noticed new expressions of respect and wonder on the faces of my peers.

Despite my newly recognised talent for Maths and a presumably left-brained faculty, I was in fact an imaginative and creative child. So much so that I often invented stories and persuaded others to believe them. So convinced were they of the truth of the story, that it would become an embarrassment to me.

I once had as many as ten M.K.'s following me around amongst the shoulder-high *tundwa,* (a plant with a single stalk, leaves extending directly there-from and fruit in a glossy red sachet growing up from the root level). We were looking for a mysterious "bush house" I had discovered. The fictitious bush house was actually a clearing in the tundwa (something like the mysterious flattened fields seen in England).

I embellished the discovery by making my disciples believe that I had seen strange people there who spoke a foreign language. I recall pronouncing the word for "bush house" as "cushion prounce" in the language of which I had miraculously picked up a smattering in just a few minutes.

My followers, some of whom, I think, enjoyed pretending belief, told one of the teachers about another of my exciting discoveries sending her on a fruitless search for jewels I had allegedly uncovered in the African bush.

Harston taught us painting in water colours ensuring we understood perspective as well as light and shade. We were able to paint acceptable pictures of the magnificent forest trees that grew so prolifically in our natural world of art. Love of water colours persisted, so that years later I selected a set of water colours by a Cape artist, as a twenty one year service award from my employer.

Lyndon Hess was a science graduate who enlivened our biology and physical science lessons by such memorable experiments as operating on an anaesthetised frog. As I recall, the heart beat for 20 minutes after separation from the body.

To prove the speed of sound he led us all up to an adjacent plain where the lack of shrubbery and trees permitted us to see for several kilometres. We divided into two groups each situated a measured distance apart. A smoky blank was fired by one group. The second group clicked on the stop watch on sighting the smoke and clicked off on hearing the report. Ignoring the speed of light, the interval in relation to the measured distance provided accurate proof of the speed of sound.

Hess was more than a theoretician. He erected the wind-charger for electricity and installed a 'ram' for water supply carefully demonstrating to us, the use of the elasticity of compressed air to lift the water up to the school tanks. This clever use of air pressure and gravity avoiding fuel or other energy, has always seemed to me to come close to the mythical notion of perpetual motion.

Unfortunately, Lyndon Hess like the rest of us was only human. He had a violent temper which drove him to thrash wayward school boys though I, surprisingly, escaped his wrath. On the playground he once laid into a native servant, Kakoma by name, for allowing birds to devour some food placed in the sun to dry. Sadly I came across an Internet website recently, on which a former Sakeji pupil refers to this reputation.

When recording laudable characteristics and unfortunate frailties as honestly as possible, it is only fair to remind readers of the extremely difficult tropical conditions in which these brave volunteers had to operate. Their talents could have earned them comfortable and even illustrious careers back home.

We loved the visits to the river on Wednesday and Saturday afternoons. Swimming in the crystal clear water, playing with the canoe upstream, braving the floods in season and even the occasional excitement of being chased by a very large snake, were all part of the wonderful recreation afforded by the river.

Wyn Nightingale, a little older than me, was the Head's daughter. A great reader and bright, I recall her attraction for British magazines, pages of the London Illustrated News and romantic stories about British royalty. Her interest in romance was not limited to sentimental stories of princesses and their spectacular marriages. She wanted to know a bit more about the facts of life including such biological questions as where babies came from.

Wyn knew exactly what she was about when, in her father's scripture class, dealing with an Old Testament story, she asked him for the meaning of the Bible words "he went in unto her". I myself had a pretty good idea by this time.

Her father said, with just a flush of redness in his serious face "it means he married her". The fact that, as the story then went on to record, God was mightily displeased with the man for "marrying" the lady, was not explained nor did the rest of the class have any more questions on a subject which was clearly off limits.

Wyn who later became a medical doctor had, of course, known the answer all along and was perhaps a little closer to adulthood than the establishment was comfortable with.
During one of our swimming sessions at the river. Wyn undertook some private research into the male anatomy. She would jump off the diving board and land in the water deliberately next to one of the older boys, then cling to him with her legs clasping his body, all under the water of course. Alas the water was so clear as to conceal nothing.

Just after she targeted me to join in this stimulating scientific project, her father became curious and ordered her to stop "doing that", which made it sound awfully heinous and unmentionable. That did not stop her asking "doing what?" To which she received no answer.

Though not on the Sakeji curriculum, this was all a very exciting and educational project for me and also, perhaps, a study in incipient puberty, parental embarrassment, and the natural instincts of pleasure, to which missionary kids were in no way immune.

It was on one of these swimming days that young Stephen Fisher (yet another of the clan) who was adept at tree climbing, fell off a branch with his hand stinging from bristles collected by touching a huge caterpillar. Nightingale spotted the creature on a horizontal branch and himself climbed along the branch towards the creature.

As related elsewhere, he pulled himself the overhanging branch hand over hand with his face peering upwards towards the 15 centimetre monster. The caterpillar suddenly shot a jet of inky black solution directly at his face. The liquid spread all over his glasses which he was fortunately wearing. He let go of the branch and dropped to the ground as quickly as Stephen had done.

During one of the shorter school holidays when Eleanor and I could not go home (the four week journey exceeding the length of the holiday), Harston arranged for Eleanor and I to travel in a hammock to Kalene hill, the nearest mission hospital 17 kms away. She handed us a cake tin with instructions to give it to Sister McGregor. A bit shyer now, we still enjoyed each other's company.

Eleanor, who always seemed to have the most initiative, asked:

"What do you think is inside the cake tin?"
"I suppose it's a cake," I said.
"Yes but what kind of a cake, why don't you open it?"
"No, its for Sister McGregor."
"How will she know we opened it?"

I prised it open to see a delectable creation with colourful "hundreds and thousands" sprinkled all over the appetising white icing. Our mouths watered. We were suddenly hungry - actually ravenous.

We rationalised that Harston had said the tin was for Sister, but surely she meant us to have the cake for tea. If we had some of our tea now surely that would be alright. The fast flowing saliva must have addled my brain for, in a moment or two, I could not remember exactly what Harston had said. We each had a delicious chunk. Then we had to smooth off the gap to a proper wedge shape by eating the rough edges. Before long there was only a small piece left. It was no good taking that to Sister. We had best just return the tin as instructed. Luckily for me Kelly was gone and when she heard about it, dear Miss Harston actually had a giggle behind her hand.

Food at boarding school was simple and adequate. Breakfast consisted of

porridge followed by two browned rice cakes served with a ration of marmite and then toast and marmalade. For a change some of us would save the marmite to put on the toast instead of marmalade.
Lunch and supper were more substantial meals, a tribute to the resourcefulness of Edith Nightingale and Ruth Hess considering the wilderness location and remoteness of supplies.

My pet hate was suet pudding. Somehow it was always cold, greasy and a little stale. Complaints about food were not welcome. One was supposed to focus the mind and swallow while keeping a stiff upper lip in true British style.

One day we were served a good looking soup with a thick floating crust of dried tomato decorated with white cheesy looking crescents. The soup tasted excellent until someone discovered that the white crescents in the crust were actually maggots. They were pretty dead by now, though one boy said he saw one of them move. The tomatoes had been sun-dried on straw mats laid on the playground and flies had found them a superb egg-laying location.

In the tropical heat many unpleasant aspects of nature develop fast, so we had a protein supplement for our soup. A few pupils complained, and received from Miss Nightingale a homily about the poor hungry children in Europe suffering in World War II conditions. Someone muttered *sotto voce,* that they would gladly send their bowl of soup to Europe in that case.

The largest classroom boasting a wind-up clock and upright piano, served as the main hall where the school day began with assembly and where we sang a hymn or two, received any special announcements and then went to our classrooms.

One day the initial and name "J and Nel" were discovered scratched on the surface of the piano. Joan Arnot and Nel Hoyte were known by all to be very close friends, often giggling at some secret joke. However they denied all knowledge of the deed. No one owned up despite dire warnings issued by the staff. After a council of war the teachers made us all write the initials on a piece of paper to enable comparison of handwriting. Predictably one pupil was immediately eliminated for a poorly written 'N' and no culprit was found.

The war council then announced that we would then all be treated as equally guilty and accordingly all have to be punished.

The punishment was quite lenient, almost enjoyable. We had to pull up long grass which came away in clods of earth. Soon it became a game of swinging the clods and releasing them as "bombs" onto a pile or at each other. The culprit was never identified.

On Saturdays the procedure after assembly included "penny for Sunday", an opportunity to have your parents' account charged with a penny which would be given to you to place in the collection box of the church assembly based at Hillwood farm.

One could also at the same time, draw pocket money for spending at the Fisher's trading store to which we walked on some Saturdays. The store was an interesting place for those who had never seen a shop, though there was little merchandise of appeal to children.

Sunday mornings the whole school would walk to Hillwood farm clad in their best clothes. We strolled along the two track motor road past Fisher's coffee orchard and past the cottage of Mr and Mrs Carlias. Carlias managed the trading store.

Our arrival at Hillwood was invariably announced by the strident cry of a gaggle of geese. The friendly blue-bottomed monkey chained to a large tree in the front garden would welcome us by performing his routine of antics, shinning up the tree and leaping from bough to bough.

The little chapel was simply furnished, the forward section of seats forming a square surrounding the table of emblems. More rows of seats filled the rear for those not in fellowship.

Most of the service was conducted in Lunda and usually the Sakeji head would preach a devotional message in English.

On Empire Day, we would gather around the school flagpole and one of the senior boys would hoist the Union Jack for a moment of ceremonial allegiance to the Sovereign. To Hess's credit this custom persisted after he succeeded as head despite his American origin.

He showed similar cooperation with British tradition in requiring his own family at Sakeji to use both knife and fork at the table rather than the American custom of discarding the knife once the serving had been cut.

Lighting in the dormitories was provided by paraffin lamps usually with a long glass stem. Discovering that roasted crickets tasted good, resulted in going outside after dark with a jug of water and a paraffin lamp. Water was poured down a cricket hole forcing it to the surface. The wick of the lamp would be turned up giving a splendid if smoky flame and the cricket skewered on a sharp stick would be held over the flame until done to a turn. For most, the chicken flavoured morsel was good fun and better than flying ants, while a few did it merely for the sake of bravado.

Retiring to bed after prayer, meant dropping the mosquito net hanging from the four posts and tucking it in under the mattress. The familiar night sounds of the night jar, an owl and maybe a fox or wild dog would be heard as we settled down to sleep.

The length and the hazards of journeys to school made them a memorable part of life for us. Alternative routes were selected because of flooding, a desire on the part of Mother to visit certain areas en route with the gospel or the need to visit a particular mission station.

Illness during the journey sometimes meant a delay in arrival. In such circumstances treatment was rough and ready and there was no means of advising those at your destination of the late arrival. On one trip to school Mother had to contend with two or three Logan children and a couple of Barnetts going down with whooping cough.

Mother passed the thermometer around to gauge how many of us were about to succumb. I recall Frances Logan, who had no outward sign of illness, setting the cat among the pigeons by covertly putting the thermometer in her warm cup of tea for a moment before taking her own temperature. When Mother saw a result of 125° she was sharp enough to realise there had been trickery and, in the midst of the anxieties that these circumstances caused, still had enough sense of humour to be amused.

Taking her children to school deliberately involved the missionary in mission work as we camped in as many as 14 villages en route.

Sometimes this became more involved than simply preaching the gospel. For example on emerging from our tent for breakfast one morning the village *nduna* and other worthies clamoured around, accusing one of our bearers of adultery and calling for justice to be done. The clearly superior status of a white missionary, albeit female, made her the logical itinerant magistrate and arbitrator.

The plaintiff was an aggrieved husband and no doubt there had been witnesses in the darkness of the tropical night.

Had there been such a thing as a defence team they would surely have argued bias on the part of the judge owing to the fact that the accused was one of her employees.

Mother quickly perceived that the main issue was 'how much?' She knew too that the accused would be unable to pay the "fine" and that she would have to make an advance on his pay if she found him guilty.

Walter and I were aware of the mainstream issues but were excluded from the hearing. I supposed that the husband who had not left the village that night must have been in the hut of one of his other wives at the time of the alleged crime.

All were satisfied with the Mother's judgement which involved a lecture on morals, a fine equal to about five day's pay and the estoppel on wages to cover it.

The shortest routes took us through Angola. Travel was usually overland all the way unless we journeyed by barge up river to Cazombo mission in Angola and thence overland trekking or by car to Sakeji. This meant calling in at the Portuguese customs official at Lumbala and Cazombo.

Working at Cazombo mission were Mr and Mrs McFie. My chief memory of Cazombo was the way in which Mr. McFie ensured that the key in which he started the hymns was pitched at a level manageable by the congregation. He used a book with the tonic solfa system which indicates notation using the solfa syllables *do-re-mi-fa-soh* etc. To get a suitable pitch he would sing to himself but aloud, four notes in any key, mouthing the appropriate solfa names for the notes: "do-soh-mi-do", starting with the upper "do" and moving down the octave.

This gave him a good guide as to whether, the melody in the book was going to have us all screeching falsetto or conversely grovelling in the territory of baritones. Most of the time his first guess was good, though occasionally he would test a couple of different keys until he was satisfied. The routine kept the faithful waiting on their toes before launching into song. However it certainly avoided having to stop the congregation in full cry, in order to change key.

I recall once at a Chavuma service, when by the end of the first verse of a hymn, it had become obvious that the selected key had been a bad choice. The chorus required even top sopranos to strain. Mr. and Mrs. Logan had secretly agreed to change the key at the start of the second verse without warning. So as the congregation bravely tackled the second verse in the same ethereal key, the Logans sprung a lower and more comfortable pitch on us. The cacophonous competition that followed during the time it took the congregation to decide whether to follow the new lead or stay with the original, was another of those disorderly events that amused the children of Chavuma.

It was at Cazombo, en route to school that I received from Mother, a book on the sinking of the Titanic as a birthday present. Although sinking boats was, for obvious reasons, not exactly my favourite theme, I treasured the book which was well written and had an attractive cover picture of the four funnelled vessel. Why this memory should stand out is not clear though perhaps the earlier experience of a voyage to and from Melbourne on a slightly less prestigious ship, made the story especially fascinating.

A few years later Mr. McFie died rather suddenly and in one of Mother's letters she writes of visiting Cazombo together with Mrs. Mowat, to be of comfort to the widow. That was a task Mother was eminently qualified to carry out.

From Cazombo on one trip to Sakeji we were fortunate to travel in a truck driven by Albert Horton of the Kavungu mission station. The dusty road led us through Angola past a remote and legendary point in the bush where the three boundaries of the old Belgian Congo, Angola and the old Northern Rhodesia meet.

Driving slowly through native villages was an adventure as the infrequency of vehicle travel surprised everybody especially the fowls, dogs, goats and sheep of the village, who taking fright, decided that to escape certain death it was necessary to run across the road to the other side of the village. Since this was a unanimous decision there were naturally two groups simultaneously running in the opposite direction with the resulting collisions between fleeing animals before the vehicle had even reached them.

On one occasion the car hit a sheep which promptly sagged twitching and then lay motionless in the road. A bolt on the bumper had been sheered of by the impact. Horton got out of the car to listen to the owner of the sheep who saw this as a heaven-sent opportunity to realise a handsome price for the meat. Horton and the bereaved native were haggling for some time a few metres away with their backs to the victim as if out of respect for the dead. When they looked around, the stunned animal had recovered and ambled away.

Another route to school took us via the Kalunda mission in Angola. The mission was situated on a hill rising steeply off the surrounding flat plains. The missionaries at Kalunda were Mr. and Mrs. Nigel Arnot, and his sister Winifred.

Nigel was the son of a well known missionary pioneer Frederick Stanley Arnot (1858-1914) who had been known in his time as "the knight of Africa". The sister Winnie was very artistic and charmingly woolly-headed at times. She was fond of examining the weathered rocks at Kalunda and visualising engraved drawings presumably by bushmen. Winnie had a habit of responding "yes, yes, yes" in rapid fire to everything said to her. This affirmed her readiness to hear more of, rather than understanding, what was said.

On a visit to Ermelo in South Africa during 1944, the local missionary George Fellingham explained to Winnie that his car battery was a bit flat. She responded "yes, yes, yes, I suppose that's because of the war".

Of the four Arnot children who attended Sakeji, Joan and Samuel were our contemporaries and sometimes accompanied us on the Kalunda-Sakeji stretch. One night while we slept at Kalunda a leopard took the Arnot's dog off the veranda. The eldest son Stanley was the baby in the cot which was pulled out of a tent by a lion, as described elsewhere.

A longer route to Sakeji but one which avoided crossing Angola, was through the Manyinga district. The rains had been heavy and the Manyinga river was in flood. Manyinga means blood, named on account of the red soil that coloured the river when in flood. Water was running off the plains and down the slopes of the river banks, filling the narrow footpath and making us walk ankle deep.

Normally when crossing a fordable river, the hammock porters would lift the hammock above water level by shifting the palm pole from shoulder to head and carefully wading into the river.

The depth of the Manyinga and the degree to which the floods had gouged out potholes could not be assessed because the water was a torrent of red silt at its deepest and a red swamp at its edges.

The first porters waded across assessing the depth as they went. It was decided that Walter and I would wade across, a prospect we rather relished, unperturbed by the slimy leeches which fastened to our arms and legs, ravenously imbibing the rare brand of corpuscular liquid from these M.K.'s.

The water level came close to our chins at one stage and most of the leeches virtually fell off bloated and drunken by the time we had reached the other side. Mother, the twins and the Logan girls were carried in their hammocks and, even with the pole lifted to the bearers heads for extra height, the middle of the hammock was soaked in red water leaving a stain for the rest of the journey.

Cleaning the mud-reddened clothing was just one more chore for the school-going travellers once settled in camp that evening.

There would have been many more trips to and from Chavuma, but owing to the distance and two weeks travel it was not always practical for us to go home even for the longer breaks. This meant staying at Sakeji or, more excitingly, going home with Terry Fisher to Kakawata Mission in the Belgian Congo (now the DRC).

Mr. and Mrs. Singleton Fisher, had two sons John and Terry and three daughters Pearl, Marguerite and Ruth. They ran Kakwata mission together with two cousins, Revington Fisher, his wife Dr. Georgina and his brother Digby, the latter a single man known for his excellent wood carvings. Revington and his wife had three sons Henry, Brian and Stephen (of tree climbing fame) and daughter Mave. They were, of course, all members of the Fisher clan, descendants of Dr Walter Fisher the veteran missionary physician.

From Sakeji, Hess took us to the nearest railhead at Mutshatsha in the Congo, where another Brethren station was located. Mr. and Mrs. Faulkener and Mr. and Mrs. Prescott were the missionaries at the time.

Daughters Audrey Prescott, I remember as a pretty blonde and her sister Joyce were Sakeji pupils, as was John Faulkner whose father operated a mission press much as my father had done. In addition to the main work of printing gospel literature, he published a regular magazine named "East and West" covering mission news from the "Beloved Strip".

Joyce Prescott it was who, when singing the hymn "We shall come rejoicing bringing in the sheaves", a line of the well-known hymn, made it more personal by singing instead: "We shall come with Joycey...."

After refreshments at Mutshatsha, we were taken to Kakwata on the back of a traders truck. Reaching the Lualaba river, largest of the Congo river's tributaries, we found it flooded and the series of bridges crossing the valley submerged for the most part. We camped hoping that the water would subside sufficiently to make the bridges visible.

Early next morning we reloaded and attempted the crossing. The sun was rising, bird life awakening and frogs and crickets vied with the sound of rushing water as the front wheels dipped into the murky water of the swollen river. In minutes the wheels were mired in the slush. There were some anxious moments but we eventually made it across in safety.

Singleton Fisher was a tall impressive man who could capture attention instantly. Terry, Walter and I used to sit enthralled as he told exciting adventure stories mainly of wild life experiences. Each evening a new chapter in a serial story would be unfolded as we listened with bated breath.

During one holiday at Kakwata, the story was about three boys our age in which our identities were only faintly disguised. He had summed up our personalities remarkably well.

He was later invited to Sakeji during one term, to hold a series of talks with the boys on aspects they needed to know about puberty and adolescence. During his stay, Singleton Fisher found time to entertain us all with his ability as a raconteur.

He was a hunter and excellent marksman and taught us how to use arms safely with a BSA air rifle and a 0.22 rifle.

On one trip he took the three of us hunting for meat required for a conference being held at the mission. We collected about a dozen guinea fowl, a wart hog and some venison.

Terry's elder brother John was an equally good marksman. One morning just outside the Fishers' house, noticing from their excited chattering that birds nesting in a tall tree were upset by something, John spotted a tree snake attacking the nest. Taking sight with the 0.22 rifle he drew a bead on the thin moving reptile and with a single accurate shot felled it. A book on snake species was checked identifying the orange coloured specimen as a rare reptile whose fangs pointed backwards making it difficult for a victim to prise loose after being struck.

Just a few kilometres from Kakwata mission station was a picturesque rest camp established by the Fishers on the Kambanzi river. On each bank large sheets or layers of larval rock interspersed with clusters of tall grass led down to the boulder-strewn sparkling water. In some areas small moss-like plants carpeted the larval rock having found some minimal earth to cling to.

What a wonderful spot for boys this was! The fishing was good, hares and small antelope could be hunted and swimming was refreshing. We even derived enjoyment from rolling up the wet moss-like carpets into cones, revealing the bare rock underneath and exposing strange looking insects including some fearsome centipedes, which having suffered a major upheaval to their world, scrambled hastily for refuge under another natural carpet nearby.

Mrs. Fisher, an artistic and poetic lady, appropriately named the retreat the "Enchanted land".

The Fishers built a camp lodge at the Kambanzi with enough bunk beds to accommodate all the Sakeji boys. One holiday we were invited as guests to the "Enchanted Land" instead of going to our homes. It was a great experience being led by Singleton Fisher, so skilled in motivating, teaching and inspiring young fellows.

His spiritual legacy was practical rather than dogmatic and, his skill in recounting Bible stories mixed with a balance of irreverent humour and embellishment, underlined, rather than detracted from the moral message.

He and an Australian medical missionary, Dr. Porter, took us on a few hunting trips during that holiday. One day we split into two groups. Walter, Frank Day, Donald Ellis and a few others were in Dr. Porter's group when they heard a strange noise in the bush. Dr. Porter handed his old rifle to Frank to hold while he investigated. The rifle already loaded needed only the lifting of the bolt to cock it. Frank fiddled with the weapon lifting the bolt. Walter warned him that gun was now in firing mode, but Frank refused to believe that and accidentally let off a shot that barely whizzed past my brother's head. Dr. Porter came rushing back in consternation.

It was while at the "Enchanted Land", that an insect found its way into one of Walter's ears. It took Dr. Porter more than an hour to extract the tenacious burrowing creature.

In one of our less laudable hunting sorties the Sakeji boys pursued a rabbit which after taking a few air-rifle pellets and escaping many more missed shots, took refuge under a rock ledge. The hunters bending down could see the victim and must have released a dozen more shots from the 0.22 rifle and air-gun before accepting that the quarry was well and truly slain. However, so wedged in was the fated bunny that the victorious hunters were unable to bag him.

In the forties a motor road from Kasempa on the copper-belt had reached Balovale and, through the leadership and skill of Wallace Logan the road eventually extended to Chavuma. Logan, who up to that point travelled on motor cycle where roads were good enough, now obtained a GMC truck. He built and fitted a timber cabin to the rear enabling the Logan and Barnett families to travel in style to Sakeji, a trip that took only five days via Solwezi and Mwinilunga.

The entire Logan family and four Barnett children took up more than the reasonable space available, but this did not deter Wallace from persuading the young Scottish missionary George Anderson to join us from Balovale. Anderson's interesting stories compensated us for the discomfort of the tight squeeze. Walter and I assisted Logan and Anderson with nightly tent raising duties when we camped beside the road. For one of the nights we were comfortably accommodated by missionaries at Solwezi.

Logan usually drove with an elbow resting on the window ledge. One day he spotted a large snake reared up beside the road with its head at the same height as his elbow. He missed the reptile by a centimetre or two.

Another day while cruising along the twin track road, before anyone noticed anything amiss, we saw a rear wheel rolling past the car till it fell in the dust ahead. It was the right rear wheel, the bolts of which had sheered off.

This was a calamity in the bush where passing vehicles were an extreme rarity. The nearest help must have been at least 200 kilometres away.

Hardly had Wallace uttered a to-the-point prayer when, amazingly, a battered old truck arrived. The driver took one look and using language not yet familiar to the protected children of Chavuma, said he would see if there was something in his junk-box that might at least get us to Solwezi.

The junk-box contained an assortment of rusty old bits and pieces. He hammered out a couple of the sheered bolts from the wheel base and picked out a few rusty U-bolts which he bent so that each end could be inserted through a bolt hole in the wheel base and protrude sufficiently to take a nut. This made for a reasonably secure repair, enabling us to proceed after appropriate thanks to the Lord and to his unlikely looking angel of mercy.

Some hours later the truck stopped as a herd of graceful eland formed a perfect arch as they leaped one by one from the thick bush, over the track and into the bush on the other side without their hoofs being seen to touch the ground. Proceeding on our way, the cabin was suddenly assailed by the dreaded tsetse fly. Slapping them as soon as they landed failed to prevent quite few bites for those of us with bare legs. In the tropical heat the bites healed slowly but, fortunately, no one suffered from the sleeping sickness attributed to this fly.

Mrs. Logan had taken along for the journey, a ham wrapped in muslin and stored for some long time without refrigeration. At one lunch stop we were served some of the crumbling ham in sandwiches. Walter and I were rude enough to mention that the taste was revolting so we ate no more. However the more obedient Logan girls ate what was put before them.

Proceeding on the road after lunch a few of the passengers complained of feeling sick. Little Grace Logan said "Mummy I want to frow!" Unfortunately, despite frantic banging on the rear of the driver's cab, the car was not stopped soon enough but due to Gracie's thoughtful consideration to the passengers packed like sardines, she had managed to get her head outside of the truck in time. Some of the girls had a restless night at Solwezi.

War clouds were looming in Europe, with Adolf Hitler showing signs of aggrandisement. Chamberlain had returned from a visit to the continent with a promise of "peace in our times". Africa seemed very remote from the politics of Europe.

It was with a sense off shock and some excitement during August 1939 that, sitting dutifully in the classroom one morning, we saw Edith Nightingale walking briskly down the slope to the school together with the District Commissioner from Mwinilunga, the nearest colonial government post. They wore anxious expressions and spoke animatedly. After discussion with the Headmaster, School assembly was called and we were told that the government had given orders for all at Sakeji School to evacuate immediately to Mwinilunga.

In a truly military style an evacuation plan was developed in minutes, covering travel arrangements for various age groups, what to take with us and some simple survival measures.

There were only the two Sakeji and Hillwood farm vehicles, so the girls and youngest boys were ferried out first and the older ones told to start walking. The vehicles performed the ferrying so well we were all picked up and delivered to Mwinilunga by nightfall when we learned that a German plan to attack the British colony, had been uncovered.

Cases marked 'household' and consigned on the Benguela railway line had been found to contain weapons and ammunition. The Northern Rhodesian authorities placed explosives under the main wooden bridges, and posted a fez wearing messenger whose duty it was to set fire to the fuse when so instructed.

All of this took place a month before the 3rd of September when war against Germany was actually declared.

Sakeji boys were put up in the court house with its red polished concrete floor. Our beds were planks of wood laid across paraffin boxes. Sliding across the smooth floor became an enjoyable past time as did playing with the pair of handcuffs we found in the court.

Schooling was disrupted though a sterling effort was made by the teachers, within two days, to get some kind of regimen going.

The cork trees at Mwinilunga provided us with carving material which, with our pen knives, we turned into miniature houses, vehicles and bridges - ready to be blown up? Miss Harston encouraged this past-time and ran a competition for the best cork town.

The government sent a light single-engined four-seater aircraft piloted by a keen golfer named Lock, (not the famous Bobby Lock). He was one of the first ever to land a plane on the Mwinilunga strip, his duty being to make a daily flight searching for signs of German troops. In between his rounds on the Mwinilunga golf course he took Sakeji kids for flips, three or four of us at a time.

On the day war was declared we learned that German parents of fellow pupil Cecil Haile and his sister Violet had been interned by the government. I remember the strange feeling on learning that two of my school mates were regarded as belonging to the enemy.

With the war escalating in Europe few were aware, except those directly involved, that Hitler's intentions had ranged so widely as to involve the dark continent. I found it interesting, in June 2002, while visiting the office of Australian Missionary Tidings in Sydney, to come across a report on mission work in Africa, by revered Brethren preacher C. F. Hogg dated 3rd October 1939. He reported that "*Kalene and Sakeji have been evacuated by government order at half hour notice*".

A letter from Mother a few weeks earlier, on 16th September, read: "*We have word that all white people have been told to leave Sakeji and Kalene They have come to Mwinilunga government post. My children are there and may now be on their way to Kalunda with Miss Secombe and Mr. Deubler. I have to go at once to bring them home. Sakeji is closed indefinitely of course".*

The disruption to our schooling was damaging, though Mother resumed the teaching work which had us reading and writing before we ever reached school. Now we were learning grammar, composition and more advanced arithmetic from this dressmaker with a theology diploma. Irma Motter, the Canadian missionary at Chavuma also applied her teaching skills in keeping our learning process alive and advancing.

The alertness of the colonial authorities seemed to have nipped in the bud any threat of a World War II spill-over into central Africa. Eventually school was reopened and we were once again able to take the long trip to Sakeji.

Mother was asked to assist in teaching and support work at Sakeji School for a term during 1942. She refers to this invitation with characteristic modesty, in a letter of 8th December 1941. While Mother was working at Sakeji, her loving nature drew everyone to her and her stint there was something of a balm for pupils and teachers alike.

At the end of the school year Sakeji was abuzz with visiting parents. There was usually enough guest accommodation in each of the three dormitory buildings to cope. The peak of the year-end events was the school concert for which we had practised assiduously. The prize-giving following the concert had its excitement too.

In the few days while we waited for all parents to arrive, the atmosphere at Sakeji seemed happier because of the growing presence of parents - adults who were relaxed, not wearing the stern masks teachers always seemed obliged to present.

I recall one such term end when two talented singers Jim Caldwell (baritone) of Chitokoloki and John Prescot (tenor) of Mutshatsha were staying in our dormitory. With two other visitors they formed a male-voice quartet and regaled us with truly inspiring harmony around the pedal organ.

Another musical treat was rendered by a missionary named Wigglesworth from Angola, who could play the piano accordion with extraordinary skill. He played for the extended audience at a luncheon arranged outside under the trees, as the dining room was a little small.

His own interpretation of harmony for so many well-known choruses and other familiar melodies, left me vowing to own and play the instrument one day. A Hohner, a Frontellini and later a 144- base Scandalli, saw that vow thoroughly fulfilled in the years that followed even though my skill never approached anywhere near that of Wigglesworth.

The concert and prize-giving was always a landmark in the lives of Sakeji pupils and their parents. I recall learning a six verse poem by William Makepeace Thackeray entitled “The Sage”, which was put to music over twenty years later. The plan was for me to recite it at the concert.

Despite the blonde wig made of sisal with a braided pigtail for effect, my recitation standards did not measure up, so Eleanor Logan got the job of reciting it. I discovered the poem on the internet quite recently, three of whose verses run as follows:

There lived a sage in days of yore, And
he a handsome pigtail wore;
But wondered much and sorrowed more
Because it hung behind him

And right and left and round about,
And up and down and in and out, He
turned; but still the pigtail stout Hung
steadily behind him.

And though his efforts never slack,
And though he twist and twirl and tack,
Alas! still faithful to his back
The pigtail hangs behind him.

Walter, whose reciting ability must have been eminently superior to mine, managed to get several reciting assignments for year-end concerts.

I did have one personal triumph at the concert. It was my performance on the piano, still displaying the scratched initials of Joan Arnot and Nel Hoyt on its polished surface. The piece was a cheerful little minuet whose composer I have long since forgotten.

Having inherited an ear for music I would quickly absorb the harmony and memorise the music. After a few practices I was able to discard the written music provided by Miss Nightingale. While this unfortunately retarded my learning to sight read, it served me well on the day of the concert.

As I tackled the second movement with my eyes dutifully but pointlessly fixed on the page, a sudden gust of wind blew the music away and out of reach on to the floor. Without batting an eyelid or missing a semi-quaver, I continued unperturbed while giving away to the wrapt audience that I hadn't been reading the score anyway.

Sakeji Reunion 2004

The Sakeji School reunion of 2004 held at the Lutheran University Campus, Thousand Oaks, California was a landmark event in the launch of this book and serves as an appropriate postscript to this chapter.

On the flight from Atlanta to LA, a retired businessman of my age seated next to me asked me why I was travelling. The long answer which ranged across the Zambezi valley, the missionary school and the many adventures resulted in the sale of two books during the flight.

Dowa Ross and her colleague Janice Bakke achieved a remarkable level of organisation, hospitality, competence and excellence at the reunion. Dowa, I learned, had been the first black child to be admitted to Sakeji School. Born at Balovale, near my own Chavuma, Zambia, this charming lady seemed part of my heritage.

Now married to a likeable American, Stephen Ross, Dowa made the oldest Sakeji scholar in attendance feel most welcome both in her home and on campus. I was afforded opportunity to compose the words for and sing a hopefully melodious tribute to her organisational talents at the fun session attended by many ex Sakeji scholars from various parts of the world. I was rewarded by an opportunity to revive memories of Sakeji straight out of this chapter of the book. Altogether over 50 copies of the book were sold at the reunion and two given as prizes.

It was a special joy at the reunion to meet children of my Chavuma playmates, Elaine Young daughter of Viola (Logan) and Steven Howell son of Esther (Logan) and to learn news of the wonderful Logan family.

13. Farewell Chavuma

The missionary parents of pupils who had attained the highest grade available at Sakeji school, usually had to consider a boarding school in Southern Rhodesia such as Plumtree High School, alternatively a school in South Africa, or in their country of origin. Without Sakeji this involved a move for the whole family which would mean leaving that particular mission field.

It was this option that Mother took when I, as eldest reached that stage. She sought God's guidance as in everything else and was rewarded with an opportunity to play a role in the work at Ermelo in the eastern Transvaal where Mr. and Mrs. Fellingham had worked for many years. Mr. Fellingham was, interestingly, also a missionary-printer and Zulu linguist who produced tracts and an annual calendar with spiritually uplifting quotations and exhortations. Ermelo had a reputation for having good educational facilities.

And so it was on 16th February in 1943 that the family of five embarked on the loaded barge at Chavuma Falls to depart for the Union of South Africa.

This time it was not just a furlough. The crowds of sobbing and ululating black people conscious of the immeasurable degree to which they had benefited from Mother's work, wisdom and devotion, were at the river's edge to bid us goodbye.

Quite literally and unquestionably, in choosing the Christian way, many hundreds of these people had either been spared a miserable life of disease, fear and superstition or had escaped the potential consequences of such a life. Those with genuine faith also had the biblical assurance concerning the life hereafter.

The white trader, Brice crossed the river to add his farewell. He had previously heard the story of Mother's sense of humour and also the reaction of someone who saw it as frivolity. When he listened to the sincere tributes that were expressed and saw the copious farewell tears flowing, he remarked: "Is this the lady they called a frivolous missionary?"

"Futi madoda kuya - cho!" came the cry as the paddlers shoved the vessel off the beach and clambered aboard grasping their paddles, eight of them upfront and eight aft with the canvas covered arch in between and the Barotse *kapitano* standing on a cross ledge navigating.

The barge floated low in the water with its blunt prow slowly turning around to face downstream. It was heavily laden with luggage, food, tent and camping equipment. It would take four weeks to Livingstone where the nearest railway line ran south to Mafeking, on to Johannesburg and thence to Ermelo.

The river that meant so many things to us including an environment conducive to malaria, the crocodile menace and the water that deprived us of a husband and father was, at the same time, a beautiful aspect of creation and in those days, largely unspoilt by that other creature, man.

We relived the adventure of previous Zambezi trips - dark green forests, natural rows of tall palms, white sandy beaches, brilliantly coloured water fowl and lions emerging from the shady trees where they had sheltered from the hot noonday sun, to quench their thirst at the water's edge.

One lunch time, enjoying a sandwich on a convenient bank, we counted 34 crocodiles basking on sand. The habit of sleeping or dozing with their jaws agape allows the Egyptian Plover *(Pluvi anus aegyptius)* to pick flesh from the reptile's teeth.

The fact that no one has ever seen that bird's mealtime terminated with one snap has been lauded as an example of symbiosis, a phenomenon in which each creature enjoys benefits from the relationship and therefore tolerantly refrains from taking advantage.

However Rowena my daughter-in-law, and a Sydney science teacher, has discounted this as evidence of some level of intelligence on the part of the crocodile and bird, effectively saying that we have no proof that the crocodile would sacrifice an easy meal just to avoid toothache. She offered another explanation, namely the bird's survival may perhaps depend on its ability to leap out of danger faster than the crocodile can snap and that the symbiotic benefits, while real enough, may not be understood as such by the parties concerned.

Writer and scientist Maclean (1996) questions the veracity of the story itself concluding that "no reliable observer, since one report in the twentieth century, has seen the bird acting as a crocodile toothpick. The myth has been perpetuated in the literature and needs finally to be laid to rest, unless contrary proof can be found."

One does not easily quarrel with scientists though alternative theories as to why the crocodile sleeps with its mouth open, if it is not to have its teeth kept in good shape, are not convincing.

Moreover not only do Walter and I clearly remember such sightings on the sandy beaches of the Zambezi, but Walter came across a recent video featuring the plover standing nonchalantly right inside those daunting jaws and enjoying the easy pickings while the crocodile placidly stretched his truly intimidating body on the sand.

For lovers of wild life, a trip on the Zambezi was a rare and exciting experience. There are today a number of Internet web-sites which record the abundant bird sightings in the area.

The cormorants would often sit with their wings outstretched drying in the warm sun after their fishing expeditions, on rocks or branches overhanging the water's edge. As the barge approached a cormorant would wait until the last minute before flying off, ahead of the barge, where he would inevitably join another of his species drying his wings in the sun. When the barge eventually reached the two they would repeat the performance, joining one or two others. This often continued until there were as many as six birds on a single branch and finally the arrival of the barge would force them to go their separate ways.

Among the paddlers upfront we had a man who could throw a stone with incredible accuracy. He succeeded in bagging a number of these birds from the overhanging branches as the barge approached. This made for a flavourful pot of relish with the *shima* at camp that night.

The same stone-throwing paddler actually struck a fish eagle that rose off the water clutching in its talons, a wriggling victim just taken. The eagle flew on after dropping the slightly mauled fish, whereupon the paddlers rescued it with their paddles - another way of adding variety to the food rations.

The team at the rear decided that this display of skill and its rewards must be equalled if possible. So they hammered a rough piece of metal into the shape of a crude hook albeit with no barb, sharpened the point with a hard stone and bent the top end so as to tie it to a long rope woven of the bark from a selected tree. Complete with a red rag, this device was trailed behind the barge to attract tiger fish or bream. Their success was greeted with roars of delight.

One evening, looking for a landing spot, the captain selected a gap in the reeds and bushes that usually flanked the river in places where there was no beach. There was fortuitously, a narrow but well-cleared open area from the waters edge up the fairly steep bank leading to more level ground suitable for camping.

As the barge could not be beached it was tied to a stout tree. This meant that the tent, camping equipment and food had to be carted off the barge in a careful balancing act. One paddler unfortunately fell into the deep and after being rescued with his valuable load was promptly re-named 'the resurrected one'.

As camp was being prepared we noticed a noisy hippopotamus splashing, snorting and spluttering clearly put off by our presence. After sunset, when the angry hippo was still expressing his anger, *Shilingi* the *kapitano* approached the camp fire and apologetically admitted that he had not realised the fortuitous clearing we had used was actually the hippo's normal path which it took for its nightly grazing.

The noise continued some time longer before our annoyed pachyderm decided to find an alternative route to the lush grass.

Still it was a little worrying that our flimsy tent was so hazardously erected right on the well trodden thoroughfare. A tongue-in-cheek comment from someone on hearing this account, was that it was wise to stay away from such questionable places as *hippodromes.*

As experienced on our trip to Australia, the river took us through the low lying and flat territory of Barotseland which was seasonally covered by the flood waters.

Landing on one of the islands intending to camp, we found it overrun by large rats which had no means of escape. Far from being deterred the paddlers were delighted and immediately set about clubbing them for the pot. Mother was concerned because there had, in the region, been a serious plague of bubonic fever associated with proliferation of fleas from such rodents.

Walter recalls that one kind paddler who had harvested more rodents than he could manage, brought him a present saying: "Kaumba, here are your six rats". We camped there that night without noticing any of the dreaded fleas.

A day's journey south, a water rat swimming in the reeds was stunned by a blow from a paddle and secured for eating. Even the fussy whites were persuaded to have a taste of fresh meat that evening.

It was one of the last camps, somewhere near Kazangulu at the confluence of the Chobe river with the flat Barotse plains now behind us, the giant river flowed swiftly as we sat around the campfire. Mother's guitar was put down, the voices that had been singing with natural harmony had become silent and all knew that a closing prayer would mark the moment to retire to our camp beds. In a letter of 5th May that year, Mother describes what happened:

"The barge captain Shilingi (a former believer) stood up and began to speak. There was a sudden stir at the other side of the fire where some of the men were sitting. Two of them sprang up quickly. Some of us thought that perhaps they were offended by the captain because of his desire to return to the Lord. But we soon found out that Satan was seeking to hinder, for there was a cry of "nyoka, nyoka" - snake, snake. All of us sprang to our feet except my twingirls who were so well wrapped in blankets to keep off mosquitoes that they were unable to do so."

The large reptile, probably a black mamba, thrashed violently in the grass and made its escape in the direction of the river. After the excitement *Shilingi* proceeded to reaffirm his profession as a Christian.

Sleep did not come quickly after that but we took comfort in the probably correct assumption, that the snake had been as frightened as the rest of us.

In a day or two we arrived at Katima Mulilo on the eastern point of the Caprivi strip, where, it will be remembered, the borders of four countries meet in the centre of the river. Mother had to show her passport to a white official at the water's edge on the western bank, a former German colony, but was not sure which country he represented.

He turned out to be a polite South African who was intrigued by a lone white lady with four children sailing down the Zambezi and asked what it was all about. Mother explained her mission and when he wanted to know under what institution or authority she had led such a committed life, she indicated her major credentials by pointing heavenward.

At Catambora, the river broke up into a number of fast flowing streams divided by angry boulders as it rushed towards the "The Smoke that Thunders" a few miles further. This was as far as the barge would go and meant transferring all our worldly goods to a truck which took the travel weary family, our cook-boy, the wagon man and goods, into the town of Livingstone.

Once again we stayed at the French Mission home as we waited for our train southwards. The shops of Livingstone in those days were modest and even primitive. Yet for us they held an exciting interest.
Mother took us to Frasacati's café where unspeakably delectable candy and ice cream could be purchased. Of less interest to us children was the visit to the wholesale business of S. Kopelowitz & Co. who had faithfully consigned barge loads of canned and other non-perishable foods and supplies for our consumption at Chavuma six weeks upriver.

Soon on the railway station platform standing next to the train, the steam hissing and the guard rushing about, we bid goodbye to our faithful cook-boy who had to hasten back to Catambora where the returning barge would take him home to Chavuma.

With the sound of escaping steam and a long farewell whistle, the lady they called *Nyakapalu* and her Children of Chavuma were on their way to a new and vastly different life.

The Zambezi River

Epilogue

We arrived in Ermelo in April 1943. The Johannesburg Brethren had shown generosity in furnishing the rented house that was to be our new home and the local missionary family Mr. and Mrs. Fellingham and their children gave us a warm welcome and much help.

Mother started learning Zulu immediately and mastered the language as quickly as we children picked up Afrikaans.

In 1952 having retired to Johannesburg but still using her lovely singing voice to enhance many a service or wedding, Mother suffered from a variety of physical problems attributable to malaria and general exposure to tropical conditions.

If anyone ever deserved a peaceful passage to the other side and the welcoming words "Well done thou good and faithful servant", it was dear Mother. She died in Johannesburg on 1st December 1952 and is buried in Westpark cemetery.

I dedicate these chronicles to her memory and to the Chavuma children on whom she bestowed so much love and left such a deep impression namely, my brother and sisters Walter, Dorothy and Margaret and the Logan children, Francis, Esther, Eleanor, Viola, Grace, Paul and David.

Rewards

The emotional rewards and deep satisfaction derived from writing and publishing *Like a River Glorious* have been unexpected and overwhelming. Childhood friends renewed contact, new friendships were made with many who had some connection with the mission in Central Africa or had attended Sakeji School and surprisingly communications were received from utter strangers in many parts of the world.

The objective of honouring my saintly yet sensible mother has surely been fulfilled and the experience has been personally uplifting on an unimagined scale.

The memory of the great Zambezi river as it was at that time of this story may also be kept alive by this record, having played a vital role in the my mother's life which itself was, in so many ways, *like a river glorious.*

Responses

It is gratifying, even humbling, for an author to receive unsolicited positive reactions and reviews from readers. These have come from nine countries ranging across Australasia, North and South America, United Kingdom, Africa and Puerto Rico.
Some are quoted:
"What an amazing heritage! We will place this book in our library and make it known as best we can."- Review by the Bible College of Victoria (Incorporating Melbourne Bible Institute) Australia.

"The book will appeal to any reader with an interest in the social history of Africa at the time." - Book Review in Boardroom May 2004, Journal of

The Southern African Institute of Chartered Secretaries and Administrators, Johannesburg South Africa.

"Returning home in bitterly cold weather and intending to read the newspaper or do the crosswords as usual, I found the book had been delivered. Opening it for a cursory browse I found myself being swept along in a non-stop current of page-turning. It was not until 1.00 am that I decided to go to bed my mind full of the experiences and characters of the book. Next morning I hurriedly completed the household chores and settled down again to read. I laughed often and cried for many reasons. The end came too soon." - Patricia Nolan, Edenvale, South Africa.

Waiting to enter the theatre for an op, I read 173 pages and completed it two nights later. This is a first - I seldom read. It was captivating. You have done a fantastic job in honouring your Mom and some of the lighter moments had me laughing out loud - I am sure the rest of the guys in my ward thought I was nuts." - Ian Corder, W. Cape, South Africa.

"My mother devoured the book in one day and was left panting for more. She called me up from Lusaka: 'When is the movie coming out? Is there a sequel to the book?' Everyone loves your book Gavin". - Dowa Ross (born at Balovale, Zambia), Beverly Hills, USA.

"Like a River Glorious was my companion for several weeks as I followed with great interest the trials and triumphs. You reflected the changing moods of the Zambezi so graphically. The work is informative, inspiring and often very humorous." - Antoinette Alexander, Johannesburg, South Africa.

"Enjoyed reading it immensely. It is very well written." - David and Ruth Ann Logan, Red Lion, PA, USA.

"Much enjoyed your book." - A. M. Kittermaster, Surrey, UK.

"It soon went to the top of my reading pile!" - Joan Hoyt, UK.

Other responses:
"What an amazing account of an amazing woman trusting an amazing God." - Jill Lester

"Your book held me enthralled." - Margaret Rundle

"It is very special. You described the beauty of the land and river very well. It is witty and the occasional socio/political comment adds to the whole package."- Hilton Barnett

"I found it so exciting and interesting." - June Prest

"It was such an inspiration to me; so well written and gripping." - Noel Stoffberg

I recently made contact with the Anne Fisher (now Wyatt and involved in mission work in Zambia). It was rather special to hear about her family and events over the years. Readers will remember that Anne's desk was next to mine at Sakeji School. This charming lady seems to have taken my comments about help with maths in good spirit.

Re-discovery : The Evangelical Mission Press
In 2006 shortly after publishing the second edition of the book I received an email from Rodney Brown manager of the Evangelical Mission Press in Belville, Cape Town stating *"your father had contact with the E.M.P."*. With some excitement I visited the press and met Rodney and his assistant

Charlotte Elliott who with her late husband had helped W. J .Coleridge, mentioned as a former trustee of my father's Roodepoort Mission Press. I learned that Coleridge, who resigned as trustee of the Roodepoort Mission Press in 1930 simultaneously with the resignation of Fred Barnett, had founded a new mission press in the Cape. It operates to this day as the Evangelical Mission Press and runs a book shop Christian Publications which is of course a stockist of "Like a River Glorious". (Email address: emp@xsinet.co.za).

GGB.

Acknowledgements

Acknowledgements and thanks for assistance and inspiration are due to many loved and respected folk; relations and friends who expressed the wish that the stories they had heard from those times, be recorded.

To my own sons Roderick, Geoffrey and Hilton who gave much encouragement and valuable inputs.

To my siblings Walter, Margaret, and Dorothy who provided memories and details which have so enhanced the factual accuracy and the genuine pathos of the chronicles and to so many others a few of whom are listed:

Alison Macfarlane (born Sandbach), my cousin, who provided some details concerning the Sandbach family.

Eleanor Sims (born Logan) one of Chavuma's Children and missionary in her own right. A friend and sister whom it was a privilege to know and more recently, after so long, to reach through the Internet and to have from her some precious memories of the impact my mother had upon her.

The Bible College of Victoria (formerly Melbourne Bible Institute) who cooperated in providing copies of letters written by Fred and Dorothy as they kept the principal Dr. Nash informed of their work on the mission field. Website: http://www.bcv.aus.net

The Australian Missionary Tidings an organisation providing a coordinating service in respect of financial support given to Brethren missionaries from Australia.

The AMT made it possible to obtain copies of over 40 letters written by Dorothy Barnett in acknowledgment of support and by way of reporting on the work.

After issue of the second edition I had the privilege of meeting with the CEO and Financial Executive of ATM which organisation had moved to Brisbane . ATM kindly gave some publicity to the book.

Website: http://www.amt.asn.au

In December 2006, I enjoyed a meeting with the CEO Dr Ian Burness and staff of Echoes of Service a missionary support organisation based in Bath, UK. Echoes too, provided publicity. It was pleasing to be shown a letter from Fred Barnett recorded in the library.

Website: http://www.echoes.org.uk

The late Bishop Stephen Bradley of 24 Recreational Park, Fishhoek, Cape who himself attended the Melbourne Bible Institute and who had heard so much about Fred and Dorothy Barnett from that College.

Paul Fisher of Hillwood Farm who supplied useful information about his sisters and of the Nchila Nature Reserve.

E-mail: Nchila@compuserve.com

Sakeji School contemporaries John Faulkner who helped me with some of the names in the School photograph of the Class of 1936 and Joan Hoyte who attributed the naming of the flame lily both to her grandfather Dr Walter Fisher and her father Dr Julyan Hoyte.

Sakeji School's internet website: http://www.sakeji.org

Martha Greenhow a former pupil of Sakeji School who has given information from her website to be used in this book.

Website: http://www.greentwigs.com

The team at The New South Africa Agency, my publishing consultants in South Africa.

Bill Kennedy, Johannesburg for technical assistance with the Cover Design.

My dear wife Doreen, who found myriads of syntactical *faux pas* in the initial writing and motivated me no end, by admitting that she had been spellbound by parts of the book. The first edition was published shortly before her sad passing.

Gavin Barnett

List of Illustrations

www.ingramcontent.com/pod-product-compliance
Lightning Source LLC
LaVergne TN
LVHW050616100826
845148LV00011B/1616